With endless gratitude to my patron saint Jose,
without whom this book would not exist.

Cover - **Light Beings** - Oil on Canvas - By Elizabeth Eagle

ISBN - 9781090861924

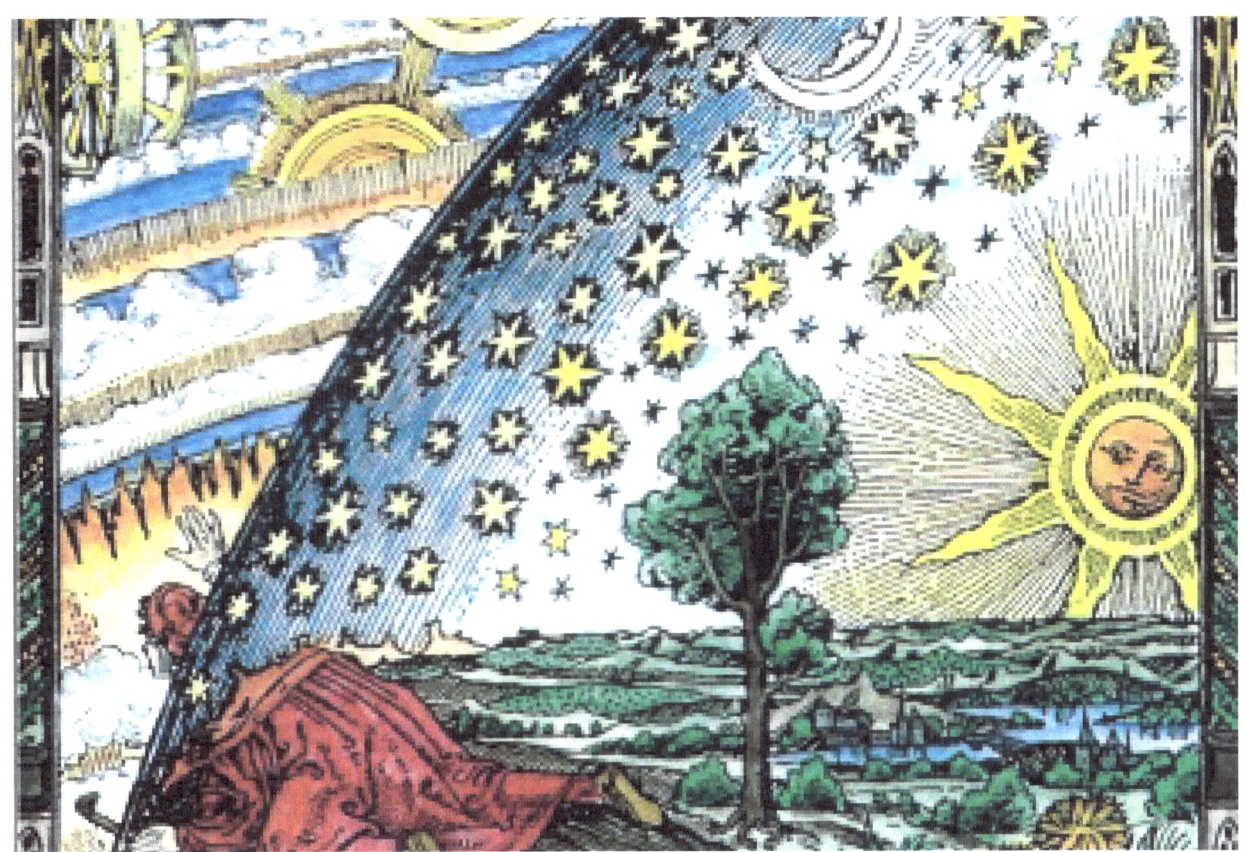

***There are more things in heaven and earth, Horatio,
than are dreamt of in your philosophy.*** Shakespeare

I dedicate this book to my father
Horatio Walker McKinney --
4/21/1933 - 3/29/2018

Watch Orbs and Light Beings in Action at:

www.LivingLightBeings.com

Forward

To my knowledge, this book is the most comprehensive collection of pictures, theories and evidence about Living Light ever published. It pulls together material in a way that has not been available previously. I hope this extensive compilation encourages future research on this subject and its possible implications for human understanding. I hope funding for this research will be forthcoming, and that the research begins soon. Investigation of Living Light has barely begun.

The way to change the world is first to change your thoughts, beliefs, feelings and expectaions about it. This book invites you to change the way you look at the world.

I agree with Paul Devereux:

"I do not doubt that this book, will cause controversy…all theories take time to be accepted, but there really cannot any longer be reasonable doubt about the existence of these earth lights (Living Light). There are now known locations, after all, where one can go and regularly witness them! Their nature and means of manifestation are, however, another matter. That is where the focus of further debate and research should be directed, and not the tiresome, time-wasting and superseded pseudo-problem of whether or not the lights actually occur. They do exist, and it is time we prepared to open up to their revelation." (Devereux, 1989)

"The vast majority of human beings dislike and even actually dread all notions with which they are not familiar... Hence it comes about that at their first appearance innovators have generally been persecuted, and always derided as fools and madmen." (Aldous Huxley)

"We start with an empty sheet. What we make of it is a flying dove and with the dove we will soar to heights not reached before." (message from Spirit through Grace Butler - "The Dove Lady)

The pictures below show various forms of Living Light. This Light is alive and can take infinite forms, shapes, colors, sizes. This book contains pictures of Living Light taken by both authors and found on the internet and in movies. This book attempts to explain the phenomenon of Living Light, even though there is really no logical explaination. It is a mystery, but theories abound.

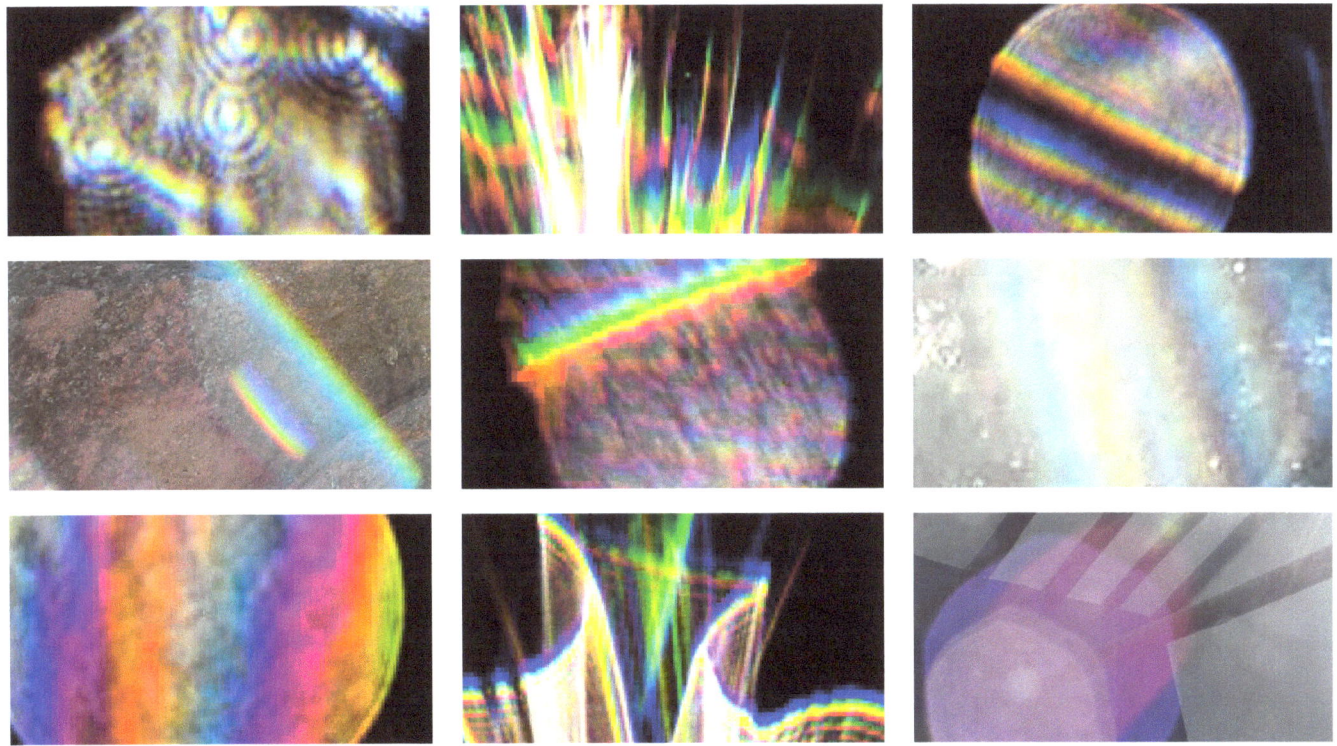

Introducton

If we listen with the heart we learn to see more. We can see with a new pair of glasses, and look beyond.

Living Light is real. Light Beings are real. They are around us at all times. This book presents evidence of an unseen world we have yet to understand. It asks open-ended questions. The answers to these questions are out there. Some may be found between the covers of this book.

Light Beings exist in another dimension. Humanity is increasing its collective consciousness at this time. Individuals are expanding their awareness and their consciousness, which affects every one of us. Many people are unaware that other dimensions exist. They've been taught to fear the paranormal and anything that threatens their belief systems. The paranormal is misunderstood and shrouded in fear. This fear hinders open-mindedness. Paranormal relates to events or phenomena that are beyond the scope of normal scientific understanding. Living Light is paranormal, but that's not a bad thing. This subject interests me, precisely because it is beyond the scope of "normal" scientific understanding. I've always been curious about things that can't be explained.

It's time for science to conduct more research on this topic. Hopefully they will expand their understanding of "normal," and move beyond it. People once believed the world was flat. We've expanded our understanding since then and have moved beyond first dimensional understanding.

To my knowledge, no one knows what Living Light is, or what to call it. For now, it is an enigma and a total mystery. This book is the beginning of a journey into the unknown. No one knows where it will lead.

What is Living Light?

Living Light may be a form of life with intelligent consciousness. I am learning more everyday about this form of intelligent life we have yet to understand. Life does not need physicality to exist, or any type of atmosphere. It can take any size or shape, and appears to move faster than the speed of normal light. It is intelligent and is consciously communicating with us now.

> "Since light is the highest vibrational frequency known to humanity, it is reasonable to conclude that Spirit is Light. Since Spirit is the Creator with the power of manifestation, learn to illuminate the mind and heart with the Light of the God Force" (Spalding, 1924)

Living Light is what I call visible life force energy. Light Beings are the different types and shapes of Light that show up in photography, film or video. Life force energy has over eighty names that refer to it, including: subtle energy (life force), bio-energetic plasma, Unidentified Ariel Phenomenon (UAP), luminous atmospheric phenomena, angels, sprits, Unidentified Flying Objects (UFOs), aliens, demons, ghosts, souls, dust on the lens, refraction, camera malfunction, a hoax, computer graphics, digital enhancement, Photoshop, etc. At this point, the answer to the question "What are Light Beings?" has no definitive answer. Theories presented here can neither be confirmed nor denied. This subject is wide open for interpretation and theories abound.

Diana Cooper, states in her book, *Enlightenment Through Orbs*, "The Orbs are all of the angelic hierarchy." (Cooper, 2008) How does she know? What is the angelic hierarchy? How can she say for certain that the Orbs are "all" of anything? Are they angels? The answer depends on ones perspective, perceptions and beliefs.

Corey Goode, a whistleblower from the Secret Space Program, has come forward. According to him we have contact with the "Sphere Being Alliance," which is made up of beings that are actually spheres. He said, "Size really doesn't matter to them. They can appear large enough to encompass our entire solar system, which they have done, or they can be as small as a Ping-Pong ball. They are bright balls (orbs?) that float around and they would pick me up and take me to meetings. I was told they were ninth density (dimensional) beings that are part of their collective."

Acts 13:47 I have made you a Light, that you may bring salvation to the ends of the earth.

A friend confided in me, saying: "When I was young, the Orbs would come to my bedroom. I'd hold onto them and they would fly me around the room." I'd never heard of such a thing. Why would she make up a story like that? Does this mean orbs can be solid and have the ability to transport people? Is there a Sphere Being Alliance, and if so, how can anyone prove it? If it exists, do Light Beings belong to it, or is the alleged alliance simply one manifestation of Living Light? I doubt we'll learn the answer to this question, especially if the Secret Space Program has anything to say about it. By the way, what is the Secret Space Program?

Miners in South Africa found round spherical balls of unexplained solid blue metal, with 3 parallel groves around the middle. They were between a golf ball and a baseball in size. They were determined to be 2.8 billion years old. Could these be representations of Orbs? It's mind boggling that these spheres are so ancient. See page 40 for more details.

Light Beings may be unique sentient beings with individuality. Do they have group consciousness? Is that what Goode refers to as "their collective?"

Corey Goode claims these new Sphere Beings are a nonviolent group of beings that have brought assistance mainly in the form of a message. What is the message?

> "Focus on increasing your service to others and be more loving to yourself and everyone in order to raise your vibrational and consciousness level. Learn to forgive yourself and others (thus releasing karma). This will change the vibration of the planet, raise the shared consciousness of humanity, and change human kind one person at a time -- even if that one person is you. They tell us to treat your body as a temple and change over to a higher vibrational diet to aid in the process."

In answer to the question, "Why is the Sphere Being Alliance here?," Goode responds:

> "The people of Earth have been in debt slavery, mind controlled, sickened, and lied to in order to control the masses. We have had technologies suppressed from us that would change our lives. The Alliance is here to help humanity evolve out of this lower frequency. It's time to know our rights, who we truly are, and what we need to do about it."

Russell wrote in 1947:

> "For within the secret of Light is vast knowledge not yet revealed to man. Light is all there is. If science knew what LIGHT actually IS, instead of the waves and corpuscles of incandescent suns which science now thinks it is, a new civilization would arise from that fact alone … Revelation of the nature of Light will be the inheritance of man in the coming New Age of greater comprehension." (Russel, 1947)

The following is part of a research paper that was presented at the 1996 MUFON International UFO Symposium in Greensboro, NC, July 5-7 by John W. White:

"Other UFO experiences in the terrestresstrial category seem best understood as human contact with a lower form of animal life native to Earth's atmosphere. The discovery of these strange aerial creatures is told in Trevor James Constable's 1976 book *The Cosmic Pulse of Life*. He simply calls them "critters." His text and photographs reveal a class of elemental fauna unknown to science. These amoeba-like aeroforms are not solid, liquid or gas. They exist in the fourth state of matter – plasma - and are normally invisible for several reasons. First, their native habitat is high above the atmosphere far beyond human gaze but nevertheless well below the astronomers' usual telescopic focus. Second, they are bioenergetically propelled and move at a very high speed - thousands of miles per hour. Last, their usual condition is in the infrared portion of the electromagnetic spectrum. However, they have the capacity to change their density and thereby pass from one level of tangibility to another. Thus, they sometimes do appear in the visible portion of the spectrum, if seen by humans, they are quickly labeled UFOs - which, of course, they are. But they are not mechanical spacecraft; they are living creatures. They grow anywhere from the size of a coin (such as the World War II "foo fighters" sightings) to at least half a mile in diameter. They give a solid radar return, even though invisible to the naked eye. When they're visible, they pulsate with a reddish-orange glow. They can change their form, but generally are seen as discs or spheroids. Their diaphanous structure (light, delicate, and translucent) allows a limited view of the interior." (Highlights by Author)

2 Corinthians 4:6 For God, who commanded the Light to shine out of darkness, hath shined in our hearts, to give the Light of knowledge.

Can Light Beings be any size? What kind of "critters" are they? I can't imagine that since 1996 when this article was written, no more has been discovered about this phenomenon. What has been learned? Has it been shared with the general public? Enquiring minds want to know.

What is Consciousness?

It is surprising that something we all have and experience is so difficult to explain. It cannot be explained as only a physical mechanism. We cannot measure or calculate it. Is Living Light Conscious? I believe it is.

The standard dictionary definition of consciousness is an awareness of something emerging from the operations of a persons' brain and mind. This definition addresses only physical consciousness. There is more to consciousness than that. There is Spiritual consciousness.

Physical consciousness is different than Spiritual consciousness, although they are connected. Physical consciousness is our awareness of the physical world around us. Spiritual consciousness implies that we are Spiritually aware and awake. Spiritual consciousness is referred to as higher consciousness (among many other names). Higher consciousness is the awareness of a higher Self, Spirit, a higher power or God (as you understand God). It means knowing and believing that something greater than you exists. Spirituality is real, just as spiritual consciousness is real.

We are Spiritual Beings having a human experience. As Spiritual Beings we have direct contact with Spirit. We don't need intermediaries, as we've been led to believe. Organized religion has taught many to believe that they require a priest, a shaman, anything or anyone else as a go between so that they can communicate with this higher Universal Source. This misconception limits experience and expansion.

Spirit is everywhere. It is the invisible divine thread, which binds everything together, affirming the interconnection of all things within Creation. When Spirit engages us, our personal journey takes us into the flow of something far greater than ourselves. When we follow our deepest desires, listen to the voice of our inner knowing, welcome change and believe in possibility, Spirit is at work.

I believe that our primary function in the physical world is to raise our level of spiritual consciousness. It's sad to think that the majority of humanity remains spiritually asleep. The time has come for all of us to wake up.

It is vital that humanity comes to understand the importance of consciousness in spiritual growth. Divine ideas must be incorporated into our consciousness before they can mean anything to us. Having only an intellectual concept of consciousness limits understanding.

If humanity, as a collective, can raise its spiritual consciousness, we can move beyond the negative paradigm we've been stuck in for thousands of years…one based on shame, guilt, fear, greed and anger. Many are selfish and self-centered, interested only in themselves. This must change if we are to survive as a species. An evolution of consciousness is underway. It gives me hope. It's time for us to collectively raise our awareness and co-create this evolution of consciousness.

"When we quit thinking primarily about ourselves, and our own self-preservation, we undergo a truly heroic transformation of consciousness." Joseph Campbell

Since Living Light is not physical, it exists in the spiritual world. I believe Spirit is Light, and Light is Spirit. Both represent the creative force of the Universe. Many call this creative force God.

All events, occurrences, happenings, conditions and circumstances are created from consciousness. Individual consciousness is powerful. Imagine how powerful the creative energy released by collective consciousness can be. It is so powerful that it can create events and circumstances of worldwide importance with planetary consequences. Our collective consciousness can save humanity from its slow suicide.

Indications of how our level of consciousness is rising include; recognizing the "oneness" of everything and everyone; letting go of our ego-driven habit of judging and criticizing others: and experiencing lasting peace instead of incessant anxiety.

Ephesians 5:14 All things that are exposed are made manifest by the Light: for whatsoever doth make manifest is Light.

Living Light is Consciously Communicating

Living Light is intelligent and is consciously communicating with us. Evidence presented in this book supports this hypothesis.

Parapsychology writer, Brad Steiger, in his book *Mysteries of Space and Time*, presented pictures taken in low light depicting orbs. (Steiger, 1973) "The perception of the illuminated dots as 'somehow intelligent' reinforces the notion that they may be created from subtle energy, which responds to consciousness." (Swanson, 2011) The fact that subtle energy responds to consciousness is a new concept few are aware of. From my experience, supported by the photographic evidence presented, Subtle Energy DOES respond to consciousness. Few may understand the concepts of subtle energy and consciousness. Hopefully this book will help those who lack understanding to comprehend these topics.

Steiger discovered: "Some say that the balls of light are themselves an intelligence that can manifest the physical appearance most compatible with the level of each individual witness." (Steiger, 2001)

"Spirits are highly intelligent…it is, in fact, not unreasonable to assume that the intelligence of evolved Spirits greatly surpasses human intelligence." (Ledwith, 2010)

As I focus my attention on my desire to communicate with Light Beings, they respond by appearing more often. I believe they are guiding me and co-creating this book. Maybe they intend to educate people about this mysterious phenomenon through this book and it's associated documentary. Who knows? Are they communicating with me so that I can prove their existence? I believe they are here to help us remember who we are, what we're made of, and that we are never alone.

I have security cameras inside and outside my house. Light Beings appear more often on cameras when they are in infrared mode. My cameras automatically switch to infrared mode in dim light. Orbs show up on my cameras in daylight, but not as often.

I see Orbs every day. I see them real time on my security cameras as they manifest. They appear in videos and movies I watch. I find them in antique and recent photos. When I watch my eight security cameras, sometimes there aren't any Light Beings. When I send love to them, or feel love from them, I invite them to show themselves. They inevitably appear within moments. They usually appear on several cameras at the same time, illustrating that they are flying all around my house in the front yard and the back yard. It's apparent to me that they are responding intelligently. I don't know if it's my words or my intensions that attract them. It may be a combination of both. The point is, they respond intelligently to my requests.

How do they communicate? I'll provide a few examples. The first time Light Beings showed up in response too my invitation was in 1978. I had gone outside one afternoon to invite in UFO's. Not long after I asked to see something, a brilliant ball of white light the size of a basketball quickly flew towards me from behind the tree line. It took a ninety-degree turn and flew slowly parallel along the tree line. It took another ninety-degree turn and flew rapidly down the street, out of sight. I'd never witnessed anything like it.

The second time they responded was during a paranormal investigation. We were filming in infrared. My son said, "Betcha can't touch my head". Within moments, a large Orb flew from the other side of the room, directly toward him and right over his head. This activity was caught on video. We toasted them later in the investigation, and they instantly appeared and flew from the corners of the room and met where our glasses came together.

My friend photographed me playing Jingles the Elf during a tree lighting ceremony one Christmas. Still shots of this occasion are included in this book on page 16. The still shots of the ceremony were taken with a digital camera, with a flash. Video was filmed in infrared. Orbs are seen swarming around me in the infrared video and the digital camera still shots. The brief documentary I made about this experience can be found on my YouTube channel (Elizabeth Eagle).

Rainbow Light Beings began showing up in my pictures in 2006. I was in Sedona, Arizona, on a six-month spiritual sabbatical. They began appearing in pictures of rock formations. They have been rare in my photography, but have been appearing more often recently. The Rainbow Light Beings showed up in my pictures rarely, and then more Orbs began to appear. Recently I watched a tarot card reading on YouTube.

Ecclesiastes 2:13 Light exceeds (outshines) darkness.

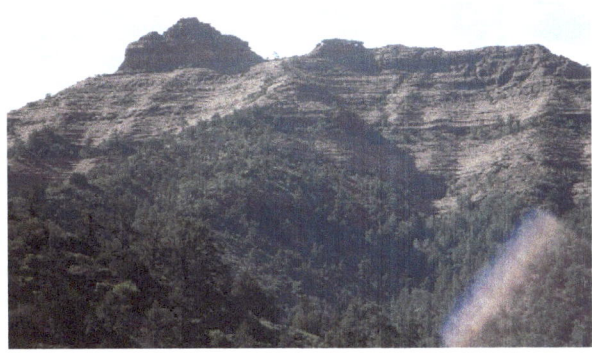

The card reader leaned over to pick a card and said, "I want one of you. Come to mama." As she said that, a little bright white Light Being flew across the room, directly to her. I believe the Light Being showed up in response to her request to "Come to Mama." Later in the same video, a rectangular Light Being flew across the room. Then one that looked like a butterfly showed up. These "sightings" are included in my *Living Light* documentary. An example of a Light Being moving in a tarot reading is illustrated below.

This is the very first picture of a Rainbow Light Being I ever took. It showed up in 2006 in Sedona, Arizona. I believe the rock formation had something to do with its appearance. I knew the Light Being was special from the moment I laid eyes on it.

It is my firm belief that Living Light is consciously communicating. Another example from a YouTube video was when The "Tribe" card was selected during another Tarot reading. Light Beings appear many times in the video while the following is being read:

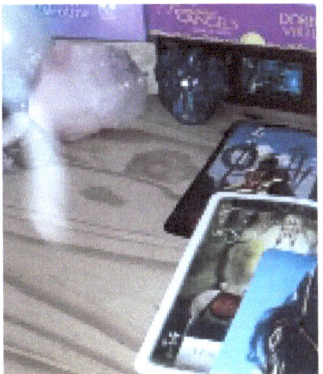 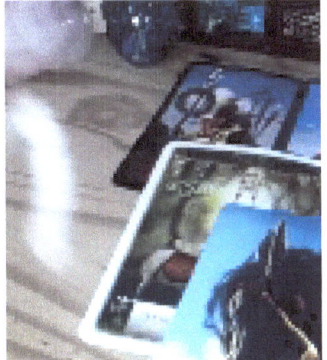 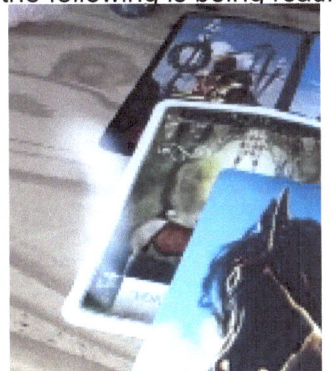 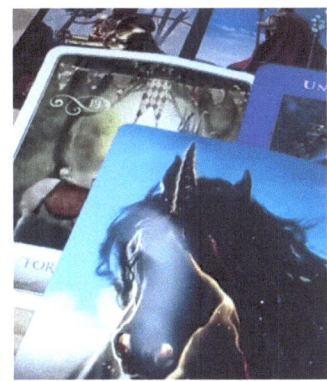

This series of pictures was taken from a YouTube video by Kindred Spirit Tarot on March 11, 2018. A strange shaped Light Being appears at the upper left hand corner of the screen and moves diagonally to the nose of the horse at the bottom middle of the screen. This "sighting" took place in less than a second. (Kindred, 2018)

"Your tribe can be anything. It can be your family; it can be people you've known in the past. It can be transient. It can change. It can be whatever it needs to be.... It can be people you talk to on YouTube in the comment section. It can be people you admire on the Internet. It can be when you read a book and that person speaks to you from out of the book. That can be your tribe." (Gemstone, 2018)

My family of origin is on a different wavelength, literally, so I keep my distance. My tribe, on the other hand, expands as I find people who are supportive and on my same wavelength. We resonate with each other. It is wonderful to have a tribe of people who accept and appreciate my "being-ness". I was grateful for the message. It came at a perfect time, exactly when I needed to hear it, as most messages from Spirit do.

I think the messages Light Beings emphasize apply to all of us. Is it possible that they are attempting to communicate the fact that we are all connected? We are all one tribe. There is no separation. We have the option of associating with those of the tribe that we resonate with, and choosing to avoid association with those we don't. The tribe of human beings has sub-tribes consisting of like-minded individuals. Not everyone gets along, yet we remain connected.

Light Beings show up when the tarot reader said; "I really enjoy my viewer engagement during readings. You are such a nice and intelligent bunch." Many Light Beings appeared when she mentioned viewer engagement. Is she including Light Beings as "viewers"? I believe so. Are they showing up so people can view them? The Light Beings are "engaged" by their many appearances. Did the Light Beings show up to convey that they are benevolent and intelligent? I believe they did. If they have intelligence, then they have consciousness. Since they are consciously communicating with us, shouldn't we attempt to expand this communication?

Light Beings in readings have different shapes, appear different places, and fly across the rooms and through walls. Orbs always appear in the same spot every day for one of my favorite readers, while other

Genesis 1:3-5 And God said, "Let there be Light," and there was Light. And God saw the Light, and saw that it was good.

Light Beings vary their display everyday with other readers. Sometimes they chase each other. They divide from one into two spheres, or from two into one. Some are brighter than others and their speeds vary.

Thirty-five to forty Light Beings appeared in one of todays' reading. It is Valentines Day, 2018, and they may have been responding to the love energy of the day. I've never seen so many Light Beings appear in a single video. Why do you think so many showed up? (Tilly, 2018) Did the reader attract them because she was radiating love, or were the Orbs so plentiful in response to the combined love energy of Valentines' Day?

Dr. Swanson says: "There is either a subjective aspect to them, or else their appearance depends in some way on the state of the individual at the time of the event." (Life Force, 2011). Are they an extension of the consciousness of the photographer, videographer, the subject and/or Spirit? Dr. Swanson goes on to say: "In some cases there are concentrations of subtle energy outside the camera, in the form of apparitions or orbs, for example. In the right lighting conditions, these can appear on film … In addition, there may be a high concentration of subtle energy, which has collected inside the camera, either from the environment or the operator. This will bend the light after it enters the camera." (Swanson, 2011)

What is Subtle Energy?

Subtle energy, or prana, is considered a life-giving force. It has been described as electromagnetic wavelengths, rates of vibration and patterns of pulsation. It is something that has been seen and felt by healers and people who are sensitive to energy for thousands of years. Acupuncture uses this subtle energy to heal and dates back at least five thousand years. Is Living Light a form of subtle energy? I believe they are one and the same.

Well known terms for subtly energy, such as 'prana', chi, 'spirit', life force and 'bio-energy. I found over eighty names from different languages and cultures that refer to the same energy, throughout history, from around the world. I am sure there are many more. Here is a sample of some of the names I found for subtle energy along with their definitions (emphasis added by author).

Aether, (ether) - European alchemical terms for life force.
Animal Magnetism - An invisible natural force possessed by all living/animate beings.
Astral Light - A fluidic life force that fills all space and living beings.
Auric Energy - An energy field that is said to enclose a human body or that of any animal or object.
Biofield - The field of energy and information that surrounds and interpenetrates the human body. It is composed of both measurable electromagnetic energy and hypothetical subtle energy, or chi.
Chi - Chinese - The vital life force that flows through the body. Physical life force.
Élan vital - The term for 'vital life force' in classical European Vitalism.
Ka - Ancient Egyptian idea of a vital essence or life energy.
Ni - The Lakota Sioux term for life force.
Nilch'i - The Navajo term for 'sacred life-giving wind or life force.'
Orgone - Vital life force.
Wakan - The Indigenous Sioux term for the sacred-holy life force in all things.

"Chinese-trained Qigong Master Healer, Hon Liu, M. D, who is a medical doctor trained in Western medicine, defines Qi (Chi) as: '…the fundamental Life Force that permeates all things. Qi connects and animates everything in the universe. When the flow of Qi is impaired, we have disease. When it flows easily, we have perfect health." Liu, 1997, (Swanson, 2011)

Isaiah 42:16 And I will lead the blind in paths they have not known. I will make darkness Light before them, and crooked things straight.

When Do Light Beings Appear?

Light Beings show up in pictures during times of celebration. They seem to be attracted to strong emotion, like joy and the increased higher vibrations music creates. They appear in photos of weddings, funerals, parties, dances, parades, meditations, concerts, sacred ceremonies and other occasions where emotions run high. I believe they are attracted to strong emotions, as moths to a flame. Why are they showing up more frequently at this time? Have they always been here? Are just now making themselves obvious, with human intervention?

Are they showing up at this time because the veil between dimensions is thinning? Light Beings may exist in another dimension. Humanity is raising its vibration at this time and many people are expanding their awareness and consciousness. More Light Beings and UFOs are being noticed than ever before. Is this due to our elevated consciousness? We are not alone. We have never been alone.

According to *Enlightenment Through Orbs*: "Orbs only appear in pictures when the photographer has a certain consciousness. They must be in a fifth dimensional space, with their aura expanded. Love is the key. In order to photograph Orbs you must develop love consciousness". It would be nice if this assumption were correct, but I don't think love consciousness explains why Light Beings show up in films of wars and natural disasters.

Digital Cameras have greatly increased the number of Light Brings appearing now. Technology has improved cameras to the point that they now capture a larger spectrum of light with higher resolution. Cameras capture Light Beings better than our naked eyes. There are people who are sensitive to energy, who see Light Beings without a camera. Some actually feel them. When I feel them I take pictures during these "feeling times," and Living Light usually appears in my photos. What do they feel like to me? Sometimes it feels like the room I'm in becomes crowded, even though no one is around. Other times I feel loved. Sometimes I get an "intuitive hit" that motivates me to use my camera. I often take hundreds of pictures hoping they will appear. Sometimes they appear in many shots I take during these photo "sprees", other times I might only get one or two and then there are those disappointing photo shoots when they don't show up at all. Other people have had experiences with visible Light Beings who have never heard of them before. This phenomenon can scare those who are unfamiliar with it because they may have preconceived superstitious beliefs about them. Some refer to them as UFOs...and they are. They are unidentified, they fly, and they are objects. Maybe they could be referred to as UFEs...Unidentified Flying Entities.

Light Beings are around us at all times. Cameras capture them better than our naked eyes, but there are those, like me, who can see them without the help of a camera lens. This book presents evidence of an unseen world we have yet to understand. The pictures in this book raise questions to ponder. What is Living Light? What does it mean? Why is it appearing now in obvious undeniable ways? I don't have definitive answers to these questions. I share what I've learned and present my opinions. I present the opinions of others. After you look at the pictures and read the book, develop your own opinions.

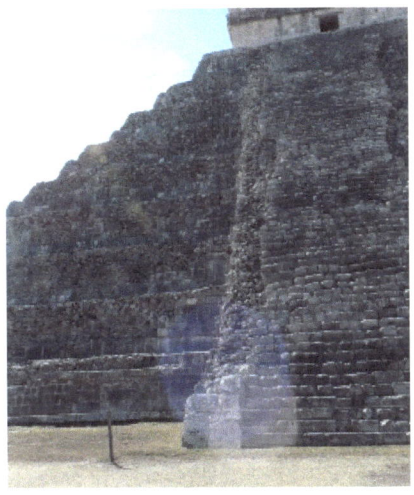

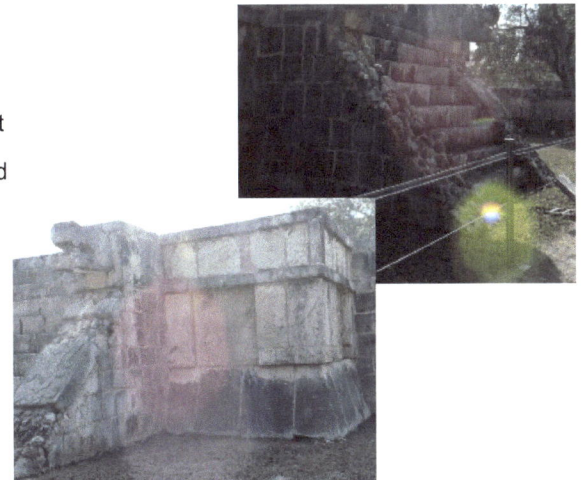

The Great Pyramid at Chichen Itza, Mexico, is a sacred site. These pictures were taken on the Spring Equinox, 2017, which is a sacred day. The feathered serpent deity Kukulkan reveals himself only twice a year at the Spring and Fall Equinoxes at Chichen Itza. His shadow slithers down the pyramid. There were thousands there that day to witness this special event, and I was happy to be one of them! The other two shots were also taken at the city of Chichen Itza, during the Spring Equinox. The Light Beings show up to celebrate the auspicious occasion.

Isaiah 58:8 Then shall your Light break forth like the dawn.

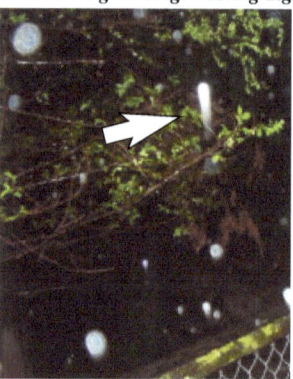

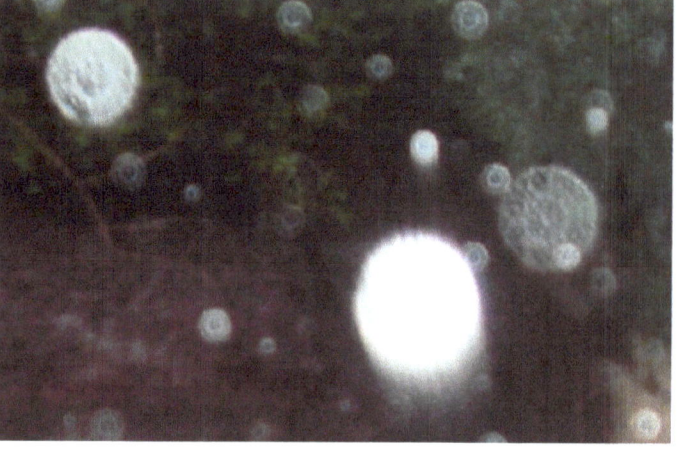

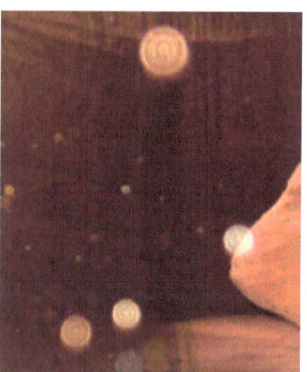

This shot clearly shows movement and different shapes and sizes of Light Beings. It was not raining or snowing when I took this picture in 2007.

This was the first dramatic orb shot I took, in 2007. I'd taken pictures with one or two small Orbs in them in the past, but nothing like this! Notice the variety of Orbs. Movement is evident. The Orb that amazed me the most is the Orb with the intricate interior on the right hand side.

Concentric circles are common in Orb interiors, as this shot from Slot Canyon, AZ, illustrates.

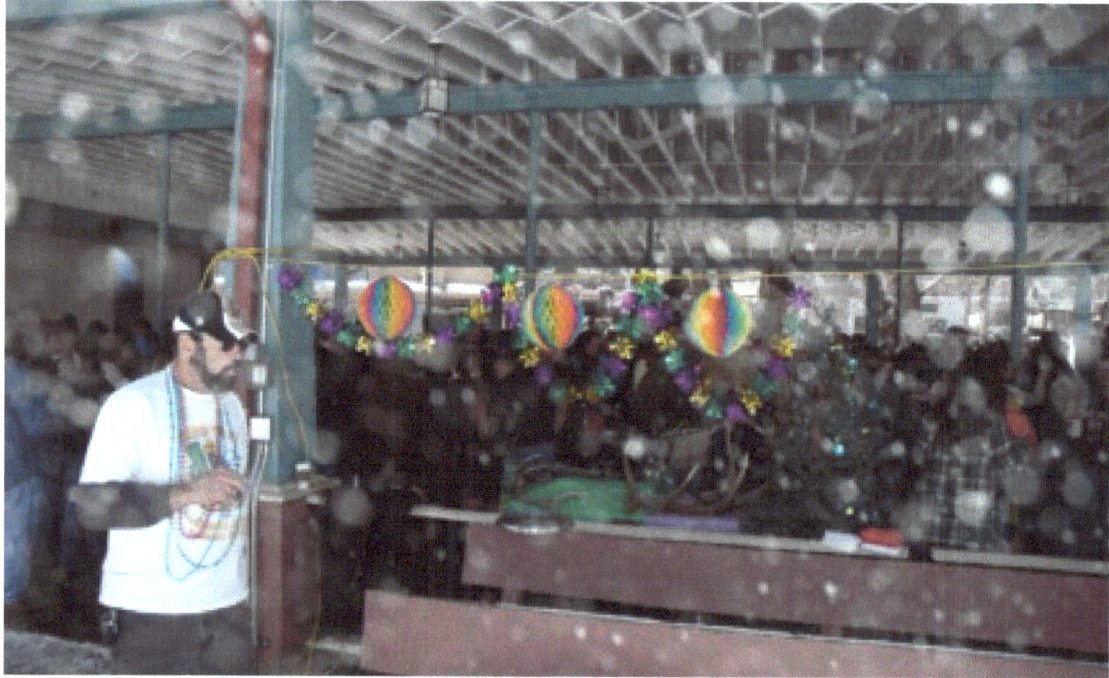

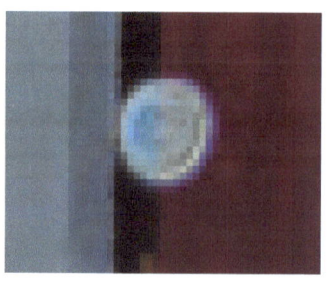

This orb appears to have a face. This shot was taken at the finish line of a race my friend ran. He didn't notice this great orb until I pointed it out. Most people have never noticed them, but I hope to help change that. I think they are important and should be taken seriously.

My friend, Mike Coletta, took this picture at Soda Springs Park, Manitou Springs, Colorado. It was not snowing or raining at the time, and the pictures he took before and after this shot had no Orbs in them, even though they were taken only seconds apart. This picture was taken right before a Carnival Parade one year, during a gumbo cook off. I believe the Orbs showed up in honor of the celebration. The paper "rainbow balls" hanging from the ceiling are decorations, not orbs. It's easy to tell the difference.

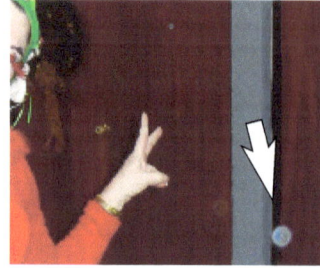

2012- Small orbs show up in this picture as I play Jingles the Elf. I've cropped and enlarged the Orb at the bottom right corner of the picture to the left. By enlarging the picture you can see the colors and shapes within the Orb better.

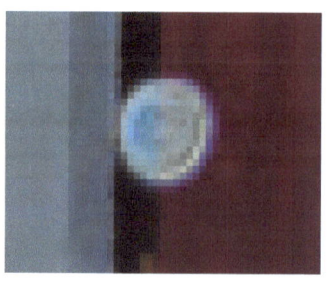

Isaiah 60:1 Arise, shine (be enlightened), for your Light has come.

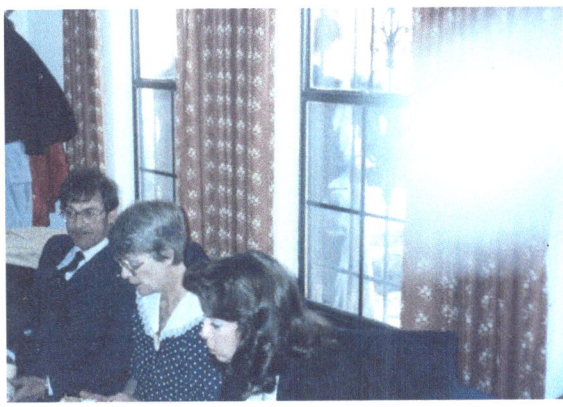

My sister appears in this picture taken at her wake. I believe that the light in the upper right corner represents her life force energy. I believe she is now a "Light Being."

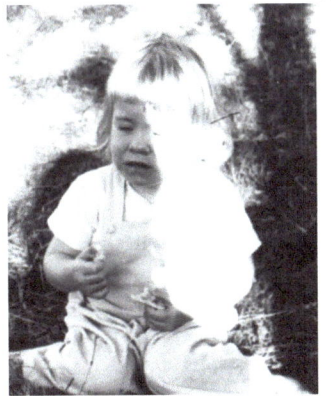

Me in 1961 with a Light Being on my shoulder. Taken with a regular film camera. I believe this Light Being is an angel.

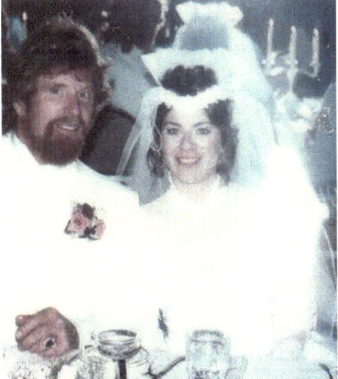

My wedding day, 1988, with a Light Being on my shoulder. This picture was taken using a Polaroid instant camera. I believe this Light Being is an angel.

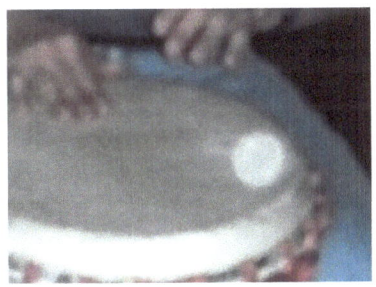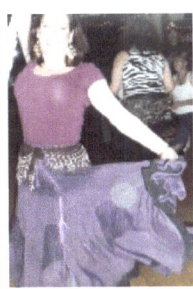

Orbs appear in pictures from drum and dance circles. My friend was playing my drum with an Orb. An Orb showed up on my skirt as I danced.

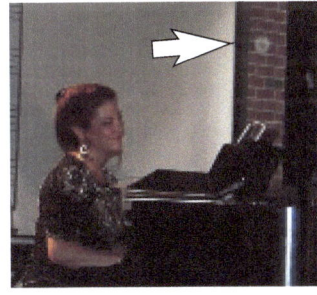

An Orb appears at my piano recital in the upper right corner of this photo.

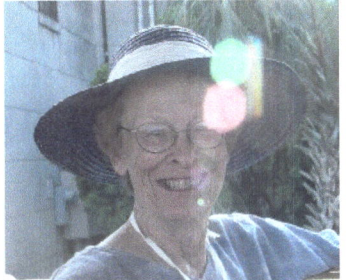

My mom, Margery Elizabeth Black, (7/13/1936 - 7/19/2016) with beautiful Light Beings. Savannah, Georgia.

This photograph is an old black and white shot from the early 1960s. An Air Force photographer in Alaska took it after a ski race. I'm the girl on the left. When I scanned in the picture and adjusted the lighting, the colors showed up in the "star like" Orb. I have not adjusted the lighting in other photos I've presented in this book. It is interesting that so much color appears because the original photo was in black and white. I can't explain it. There's a star Orb up high in the picture and another one above the tallest skiers' head. The Orbs have been cropped and enlarged.

A bright Orb appears on my friends hands at Christmas.

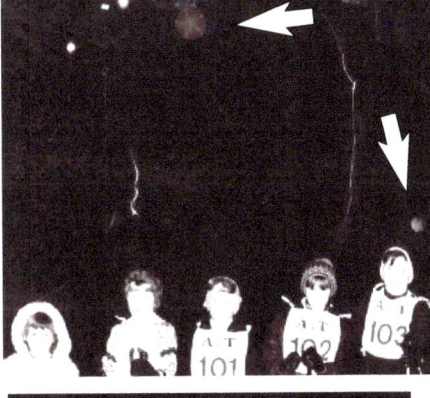

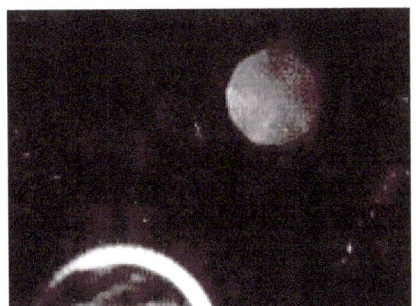

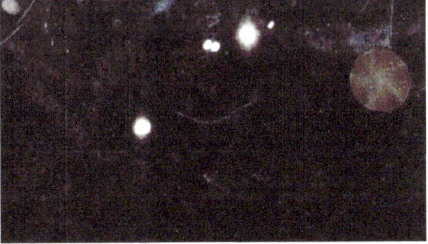

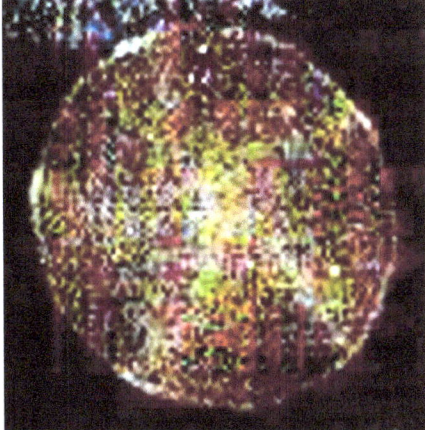

Isaiah 60:19 The Lord shall be unto thee an everlasting Light.

Light Beings from The Past

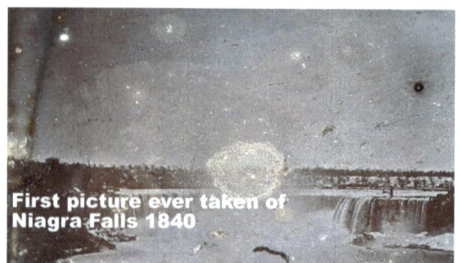

First picture ever taken of Niagra Falls 1840

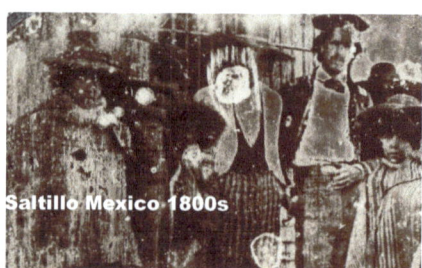

Saltillo Mexico 1800s

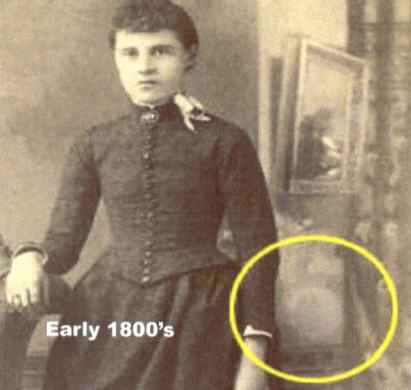

Early 1800's

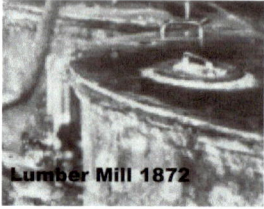

Lumber Mill 1872

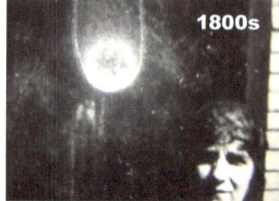

1800s

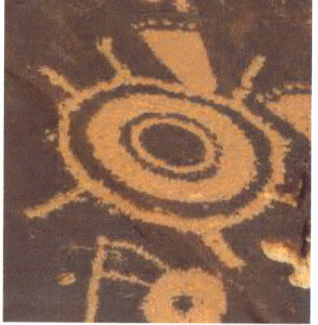

Is this ancient petroglyph a representation of several orbs, a UFO, or both?

Lumber Mill 1872

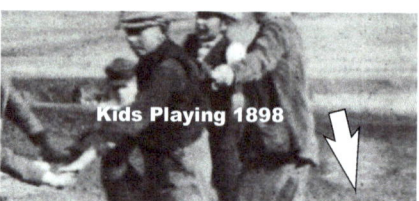

Kids Playing 1898

These photos from the 1800s show a variety of Light Beings. The traditional round shaped Orbs are shown, as well as irregularly shaped Light Beings. The Light Beings in the first picture ever taken of Niagra Falls in the 1840s has both round and irregular Orbs. The examples from the Lumber Mill in 1872 resemble flowers. Light Beings show up in old pictures. Are they also depicted in petroglyphs?

Historical Light Being Sightings from England
(989 - 1969)

989 - "Three brilliantly luminous round objects were seen on August 3rd over Japan. They were seen to join together". (Quoted by J. Ballee in Passport to Magonia (1970), Tandem edition 1975.

1606 - Fireballs were regularly reported over Kyoto, Japan… they hovered near the Nijo Castle and had many witnesses.

1740 - 1760 - "The ' Age of Reason' when former observations tended to be dismissed as superstition, and everything had to be explained by logical science."

1783 - "Cavallo gave an account of the sighting in the *Royal Society's Philosophical Transactions*: "A luminous object could be seen which soon became spherical, brilliantly lit…This strange sphere seemed at first to be pale blue in color, and its luminosity increased. Before it vanished, it changed its shape, became oblong, and at the same time, a sort of trail appeared. It seemed to separate into two small bodies."

1915 - "During the summer of 1915, unusual floating lights were seen in the area of Dartmoor that became the concern of the (British) Navel Intelligence Department…because of this military interest, we do have a few eyewitness reports of the phenomena – even one by the main investigating intelligence officer."

1919 - "A man reported a detailed sighting of extraordinary lights playing lazily about and above the prehistoric stone circle of Castlerig."

1923 - "A skeptic, George White, set out to the hills with two companions. He did so out of 'sheer curiosity' because he 'frankly did not believe a word' of the local claims of repeated sightings. The lights had reportedly been seen 'thousands' of times. White and his companions witnessed the strange lights that night."

1923 - A reporter from the *Birmingham Post* said he's seen lights cavorting: "We were facing the Edge Hills across the valley, and the light, well-defined and spherical, moved across our field of vision with its peculiar switchback motion from left to right, disappearing as suddenly as it had come. A few moments later we saw it again, a pin-point of light, which seemed to be growing larger every second, moving, however, hardly at all."1923 - Irish writer Dermont Mac Manus witnessed: "A patch of ground covered with dozens of twinkling lights rather like fireflies. They moved around with occasional bobbing up and down. They were all the same color, a pale yellow, and sparkled in the prettiest way up and down over the mounds and in and out through the rushes."

1923 - "About 200 yards away was a strong and dazzling light…I had my field glasses and was able to get a 'close-up' view. It was a kind of reddy-blue mixed, but beautifully blended. Later there was a tinge of orange color".

1940s - "Allied aircrew reported numerous contacts with a range of discoid spherical objects, mainly over the European theatre of war, but also some over the Pacific. The objects were nicknamed 'foo fighters' and usually took the form of small orange balls of light, some translucent – and occasional larger phenomena. They occurred singly and in formations. Although several air crew reported apparent 'intelligent' behavior by these spheroids, they seemed insubstantial and never harmed aircraft." German pilots, too, witnessed these phenomena.

1969 - John Mitchell wrote: "There is no doubt that…phantom lights are manifestations of electro-magnetic energy most commonly encountered in the neighborhood of geological faults, during episodes of magnetic disturbance."
(Devereux, 1989)

Isaiah 60:2-3 Nations shall come to your Light, and kings to the brightness of your rising.

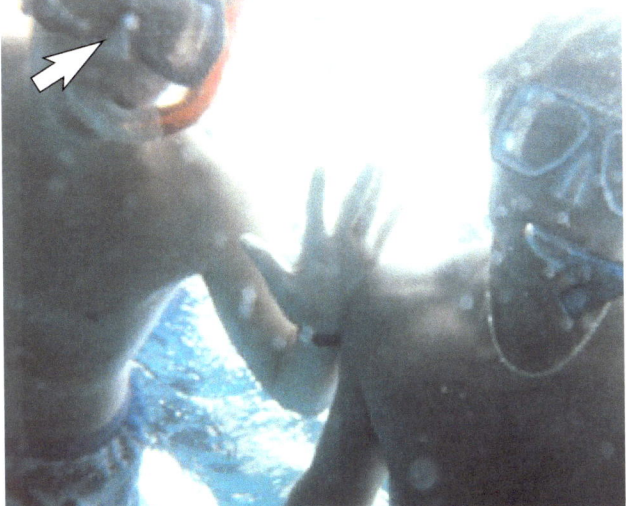

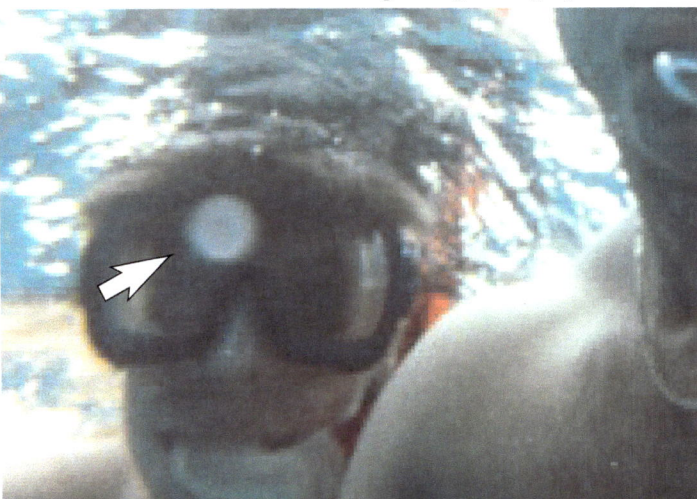

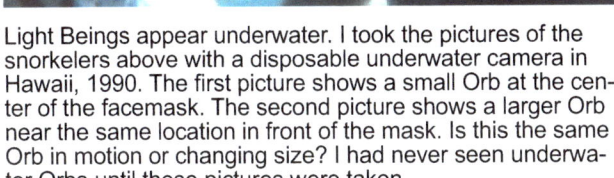

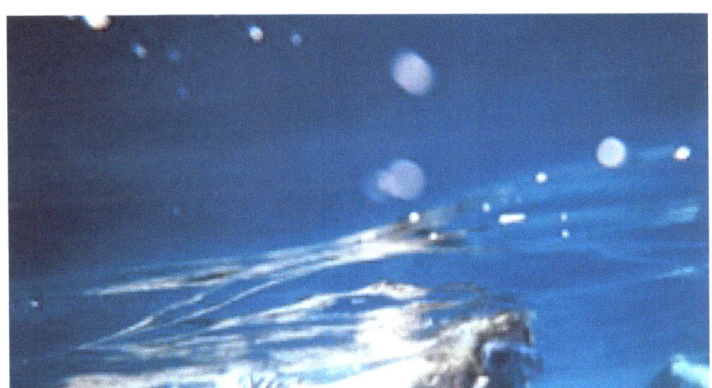

Light Beings appear underwater. I took the pictures of the snorkelers above with a disposable underwater camera in Hawaii, 1990. The first picture shows a small Orb at the center of the facemask. The second picture shows a larger Orb near the same location in front of the mask. Is this the same Orb in motion or changing size? I had never seen underwater Orbs until these pictures were taken.

The blue underwater pictures are from the Internet, and show Light Beings of different colors and shapes. The one below is a Marine Corps photo taken by Corporal Devan K. Gowans.

The picture of the lady swimming (by Rick Escalante) shows amazing pink Orbs. It is plain to see the difference between Orbs and bubbles.

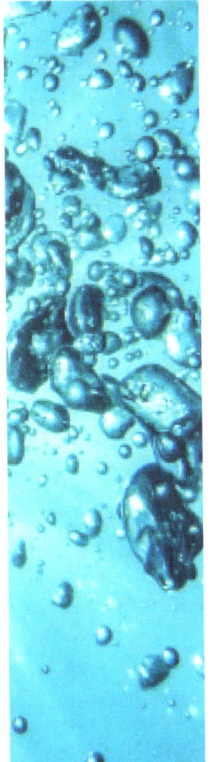

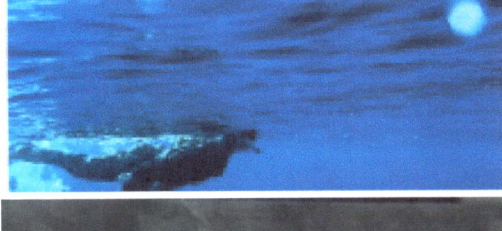

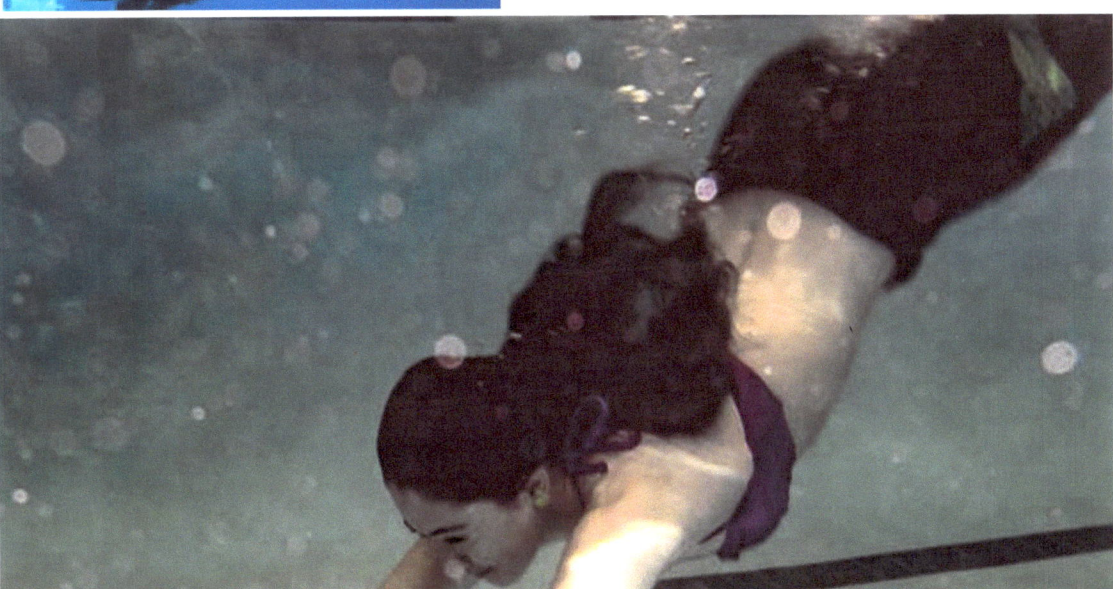

Job 24:12-13 There are those who rebel against the Light. They know not the ways there of, and know not the paths there of.

This collection of Orb shots are some of the best I've taken. I have zoomed in on them and cropped them, but no contrast or color correction has been done. These shots came from larger pictures. An example of the types of pictures these Orb shots came from can be seen in the example of the rock formation pink Light Being below this collection.

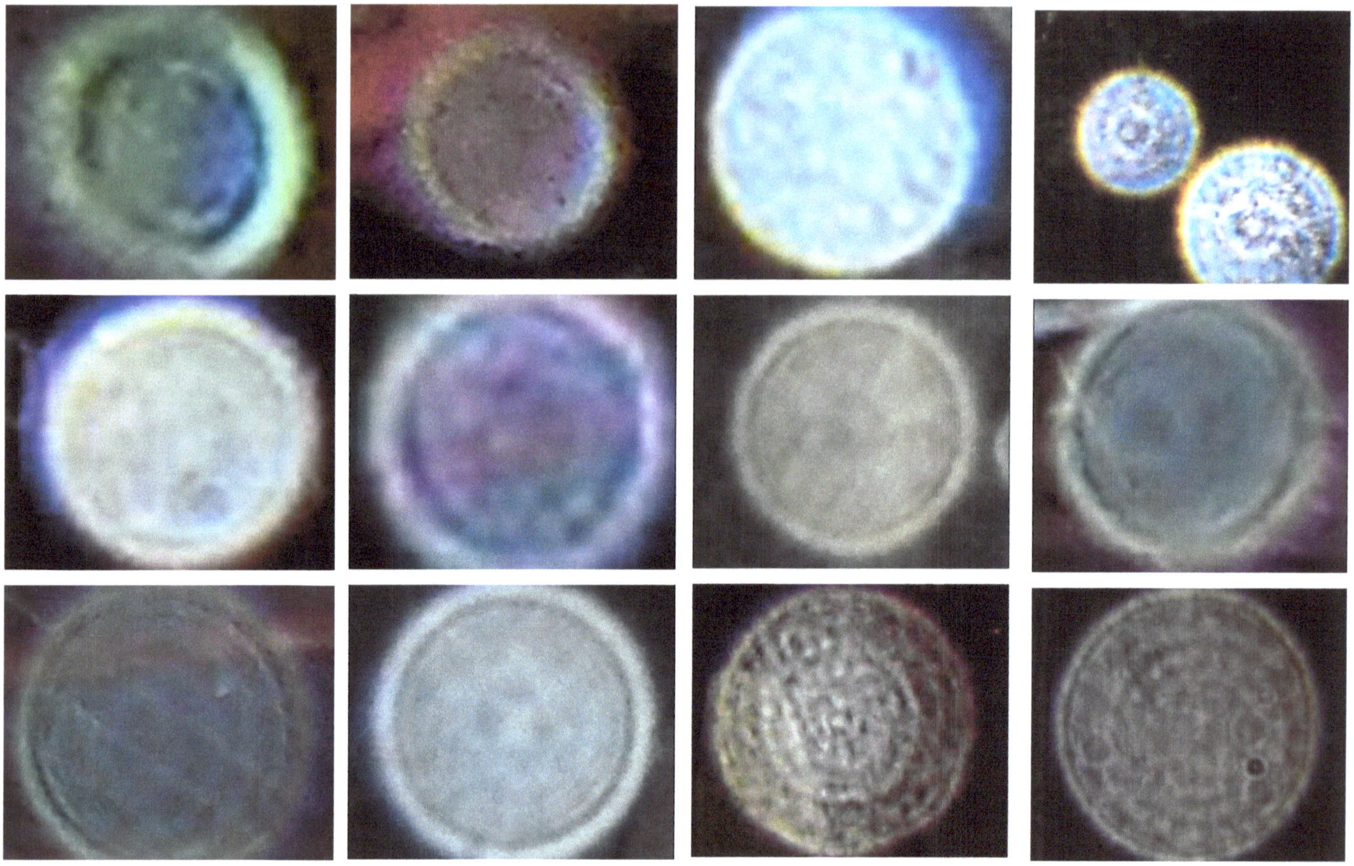

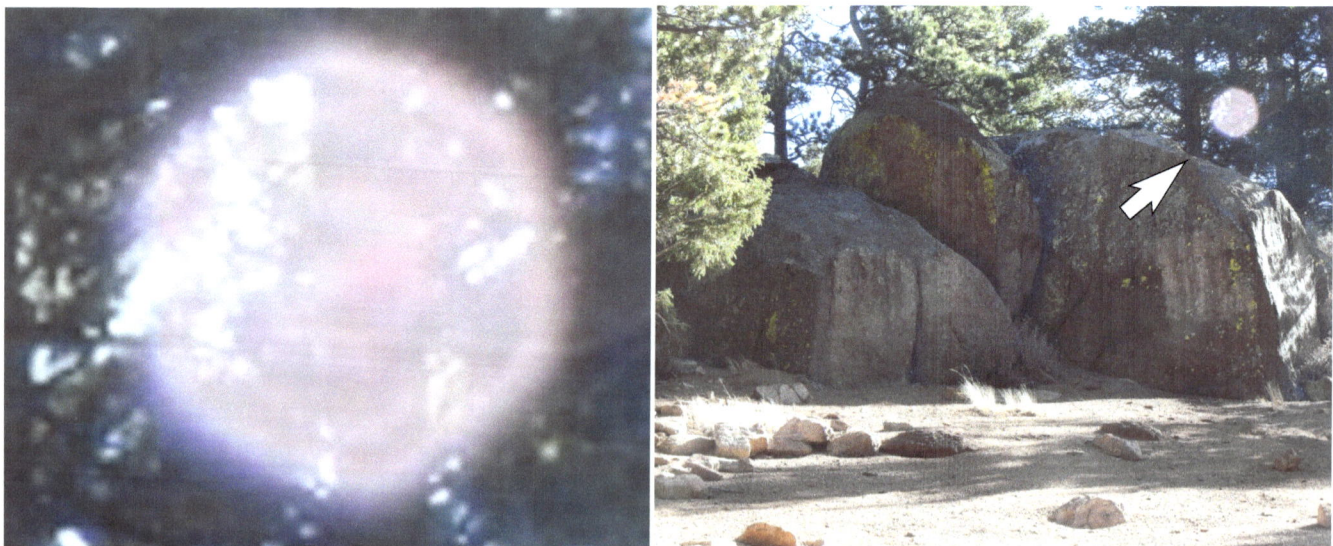

This pink Light Being is the only one that shows up in the picture beside it. This is how Light Beings often materialize. In many pictures only a single Light Being appears. The many examples of orbs I include in this book came from pictures like this. I have cropped and enlarged the Light Beings that appear in photos to show the variety of colors, shapes and sizes they exhibit. This picture was taken with a digital camera without a flash.

John 1:4-8 In him was life, and the life was the light of men. The Light shines in the darkness, and the darkness has not overcome it. There was a messenger sent from God. His name was John. He came as a witness, to tell about the Light. The true Light, which Lighteth (enlightens) every man, that cometh into the world.

The photos below give examples of the vast variety of shapes, sizes, colors, opacity and levels of brightness Light Beings exhibit. These have been cropped from larger pictures. What are they? Why is there such variety? Are they connected somehow?

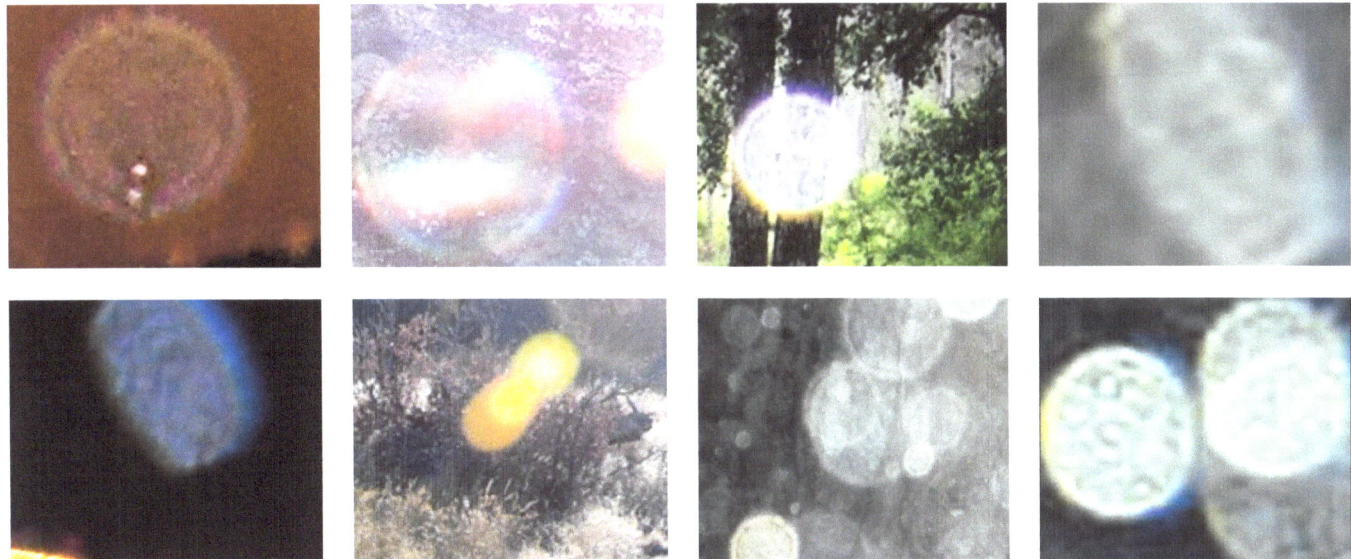

Light Beings present themselves in a wide variety of shapes and sizes. You will be amazed by the variety that show up in pictures taken by Grace Butler. I am saving her photos for later in the book because they are what I consider the best of the best, and I'd like to save the best until last. Leonore Sweet, Ph.D., shares the different shapes she's photographed:

> "I have photographed lots of irregularly shaped orbs: orbs in motion with and without contrails, and orbs in the shapes of spheres, eggs, strings of lights, footballs, butterflies, rods, cocoons, cylinders, and discs. I have seen pictures of orbs that are shaped like diamonds, squares, computer chips, octagons, shields, hearts, rectangles, triangular wedges, and even cameras and umbrellas. Lens flare and other camera problems can create some of these forms under certain conditions, and some orbsters discount all orbs except for their list of certain, specific shapes and luminosities." (Sweet, 2005)

As you look at the pictures and read the book, you'll see that the variety of forms Light Beings take may be infinite. Just as every snowflake is different, perhaps every Light Being is different. There are shapes that repeat themselves, but they are not always the same size, color, or brightness. Opacity is also something that changes. Some Light Beings are transparent. Others are opaque so you can't see through them. Most fall somewhere in between transparent and opaque.

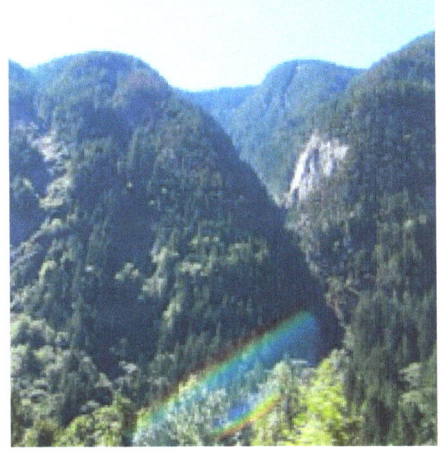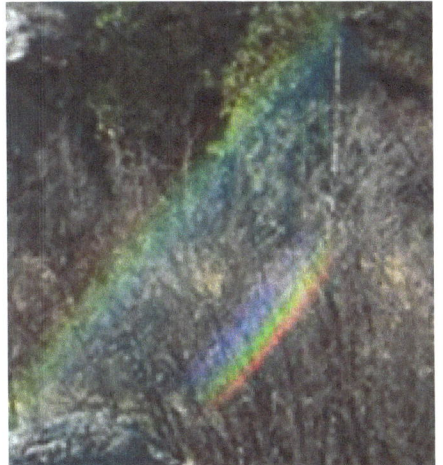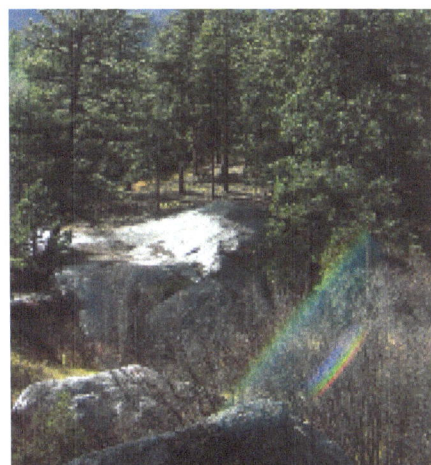

These "Rainbow Light Being" shots were taken in Colorado and Canada. Might these be Light Beings of a similar variety? I get excited every time one of these beautiful beings appears in my photography.

John 12:36 While ye have the Light, believe in the Light, that ye may be the children of Light.

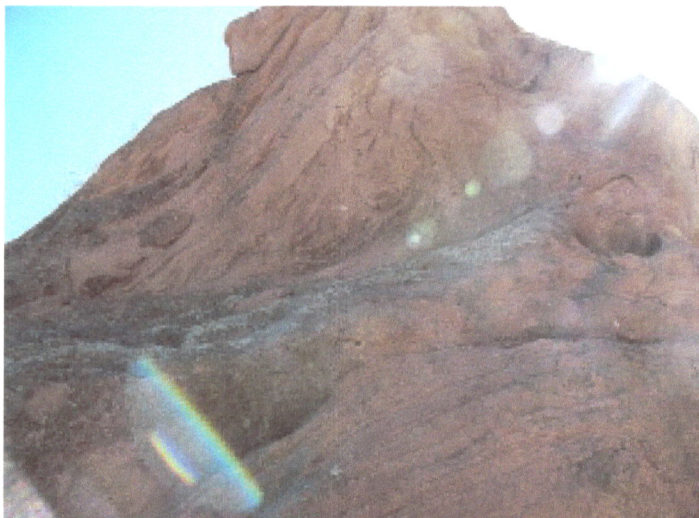

Notice the variety of Light Beings in the sunbeam above.

This "Rainbow Light Being" shot to the left was taken in the Garden of the Goddesses near Old Colorado City, Colorado. The colors are more vivid in these shots than in many I've taken. I get excited when I discover something new in my pictures, like the multicolor neon colors that show up in the corner of the original picture. I zoomed and cropped the original picture so you could see these amazing Living Lights clearly.

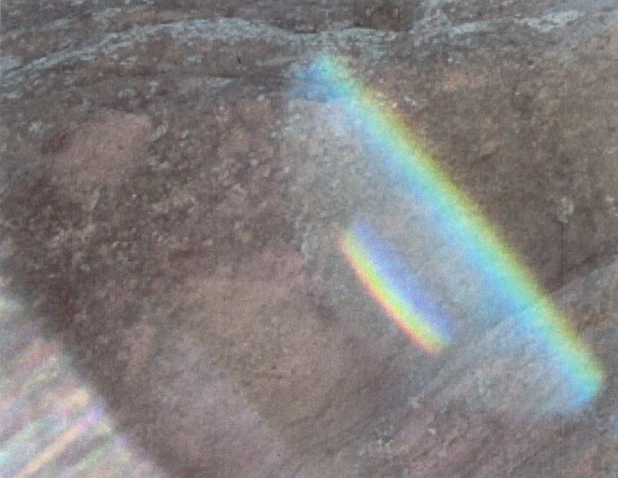

This half moon shaped Rainbow Light Being has an interior rainbow. I find it interesting that the some of the lights are parallel and others are perpendicular to each other.

This amazing expression of Living Light was the first I'd taken that looked like it. It's interesting that so many different types of Light configurations appear in the original photo, this being one of them.

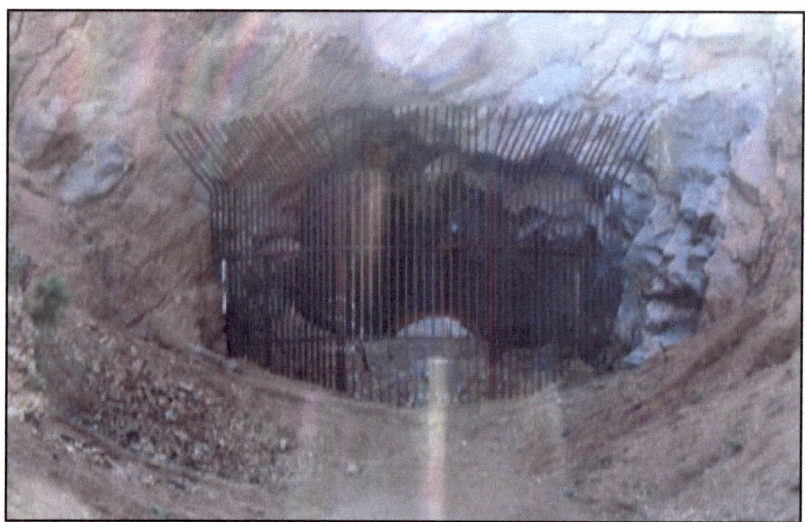

This shot of a mining tunnel blocked by bars has a neon effect at its upper left corner. The neon colors are similar to the ones in the picture to the left. Why are shafts of light appearing at a mineshaft? Taken near Horse Tooth Falls on the road to Cripple Creek, Colorado.

These two shots show very similar Light Beings. The pictures were not taken on the same day. The half rainbow by the half moon shaped rainbow is consistent in both shots.

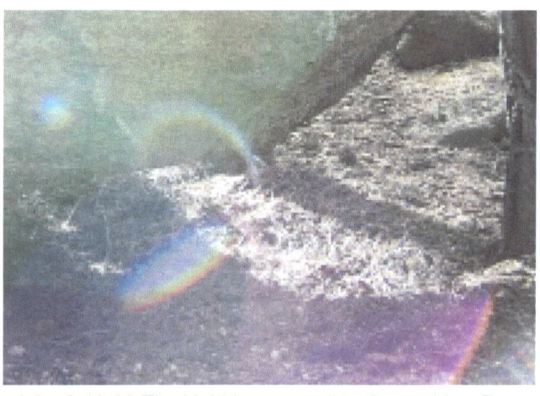

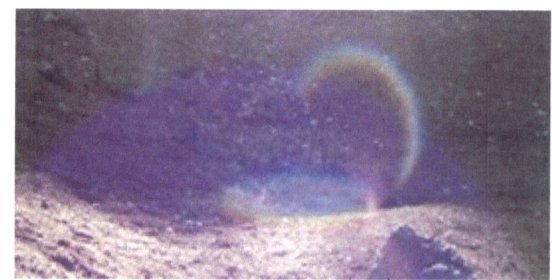

John 3:19-28 The Light has come into the world … For everyone who does evil hates the Light, lest his deeds should be examined (exposed). But whoever does what is true comes to the Light, so that it may be clearly seen.

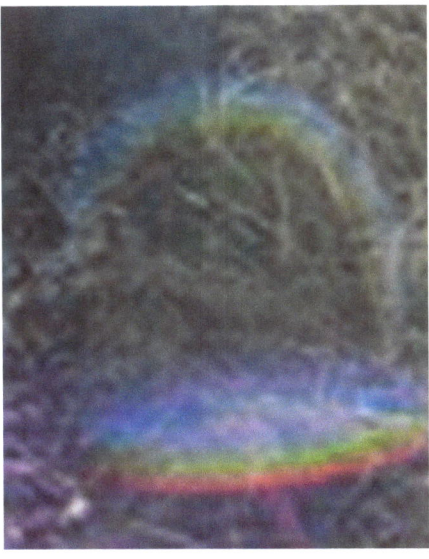 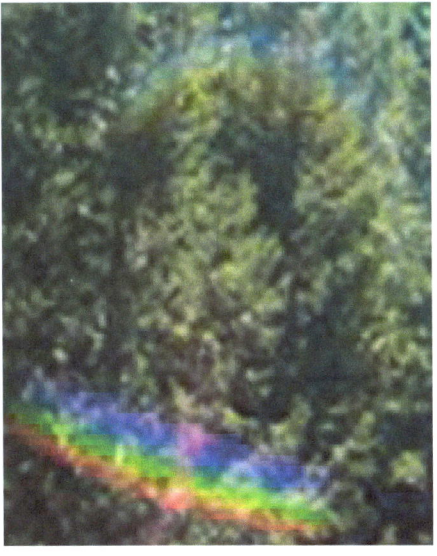 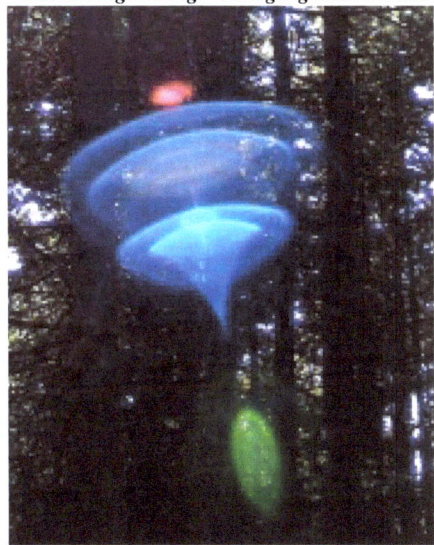

These two shots were taken during a hike one day. I was surprised to find such similar Light Beings hundreds of pictures apart. You can tell these are different Light Beings because of the difference in the backgrounds. They sure look like twins to me. Maybe not identical twins. I wonder if they belong to the same species?

This fabulous picture of a Light Being was found on the Internet. When I tried to find it again to give credit to the photographer, I could not find the image. If I have violated a copyright, I apologize and hope you will contact me to resolve any issues we may have.

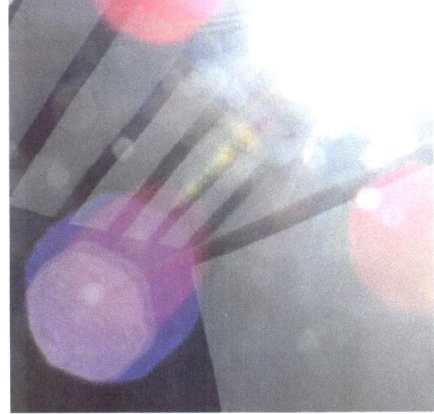 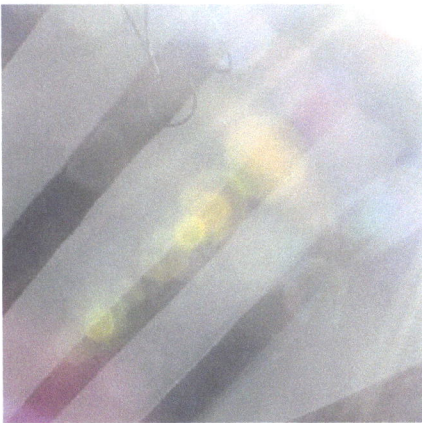

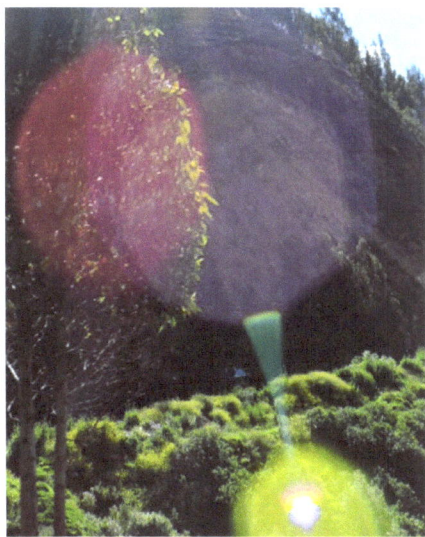

I was so happy to see this Light Being when I reviewed the pictures I'd taken March 21, 2017 in Peru. Its green "tail" is similar to the tail of the Internet photo shown above. What do the different shapes and colors represent? I don't think they are random, but instead, related.

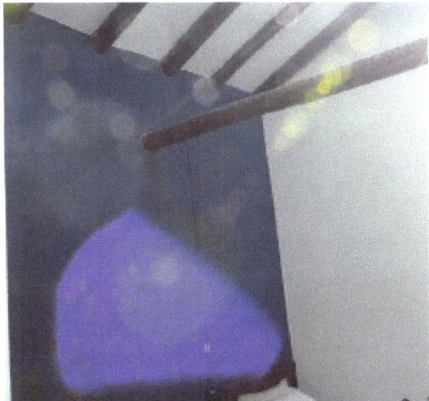 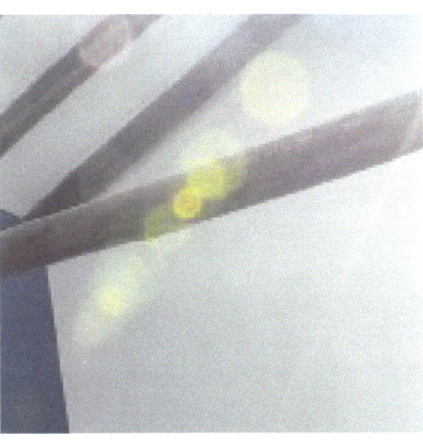

Light Beings visiting me in my hotel room in Cusco, Peru, 4/22/17. I first show the original pictures that include the shape shifting purple Light Being. Then I isolate the sunbeam streams to emphasize and enlarge them. I used to think that the variety of circles that appear in light beam streams were only refraction. Now I believe that when the light is at a certain angle, it hits another dimension, where the Light Beings show themselves.

John 8:12 I am the Light of the world. Whoever follows me will not walk in darkness (ignorance), but will have the Light of life.

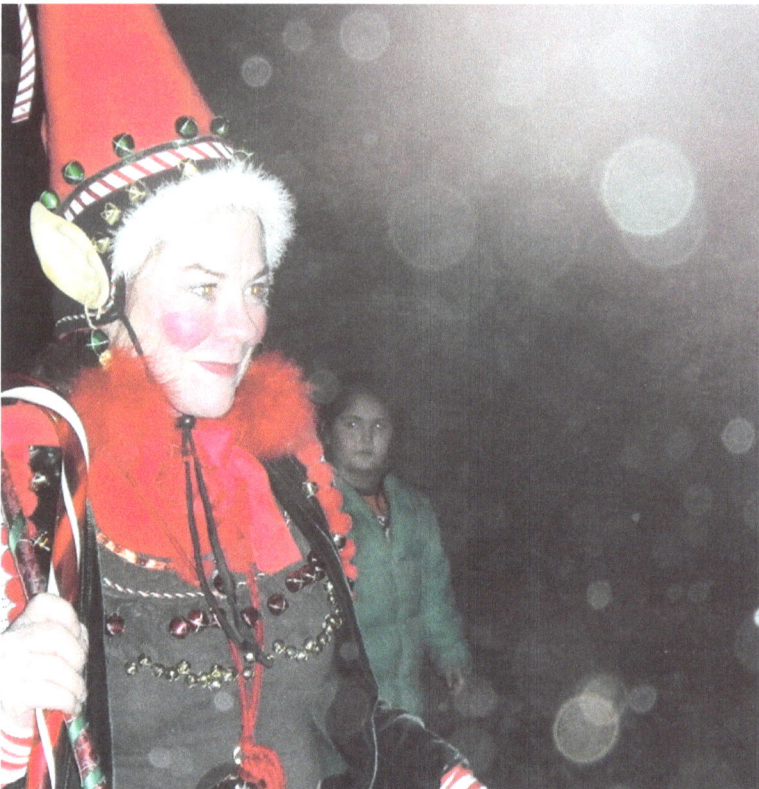

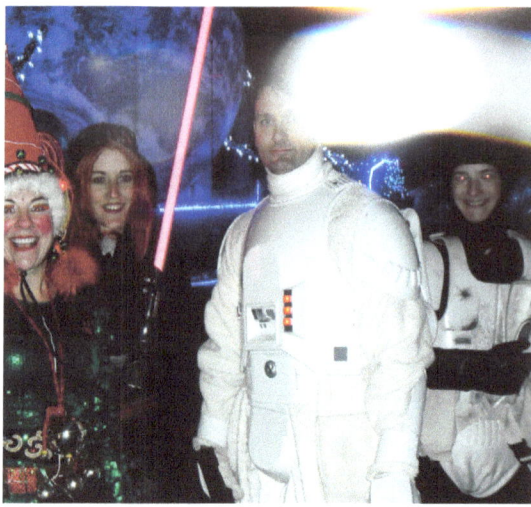

I volunteer as Jingles the Elf every Christmas season. As these pictures show, the Orbs seem attracted to the happy energy present. These pictures were taken at a tree lighting ceremony in my hometown, and at the Festival of Lights Parade. Is the moving white Light Being showing us that the force is with us? I think the person taking the pictures has much to do with if, and when, Light Beings appear. My patron saint Jose, who was in the parade with me as Jangles the Elf, took these pictures. He has wonderful energy, and between the two of us, we were as happy as two elves could be. I think the Light Beings showed up to celebrate the season with us.

Orbs seem to enjoy being photographed at joyful occations. These shots were taken by my friend at a Christmas Tree Lighting Ceremony in Fountain, Colorado. A digital camera with flash was used. The small single Orb in the picture below at the arrow was taken with a digital camera with a flash in my house.

May the Light shine on YOU!

This shot taken with a Storm Trooper shows irregularly shaped Light Beings or Orbs traveling at different angles. These were some of the first rectangular shaped Light Beings photographed. Jose took this shot as well.

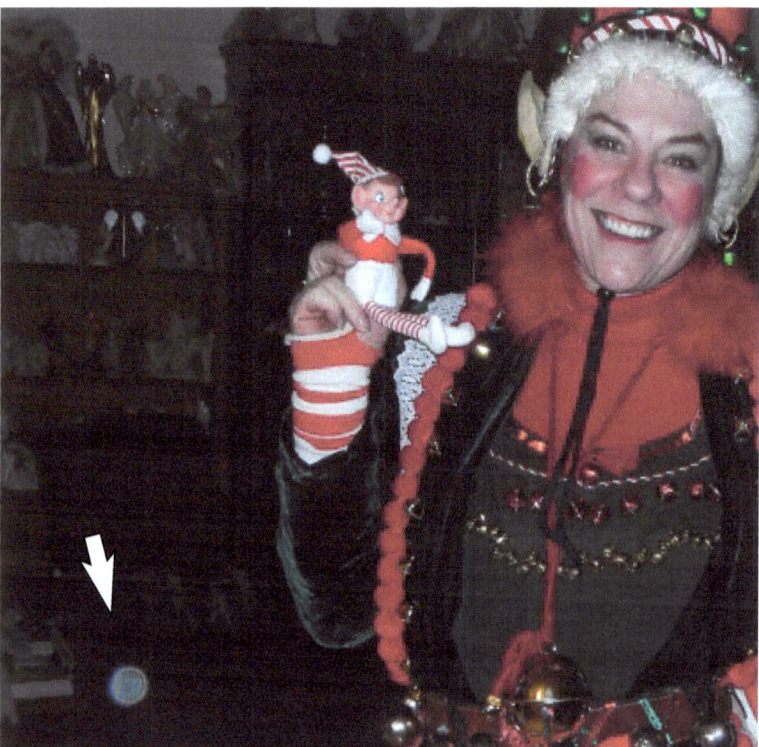

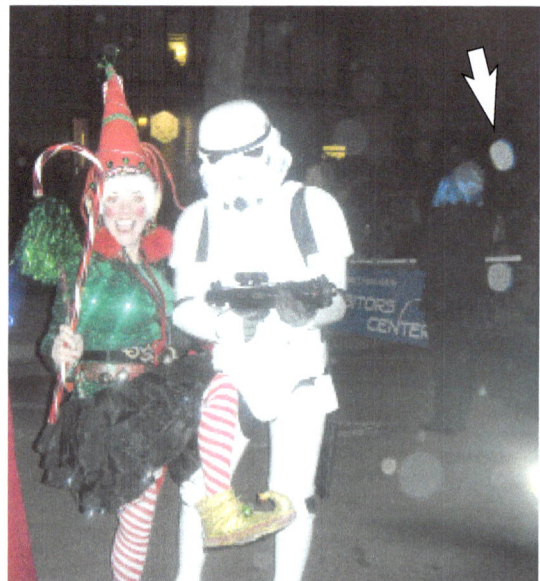

John 9:5 As long as I am in the world, I am the Light of the world.

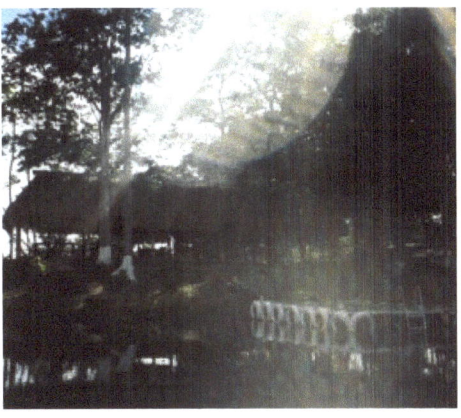

Energy exudes from this secluded island on the Panama Canal.

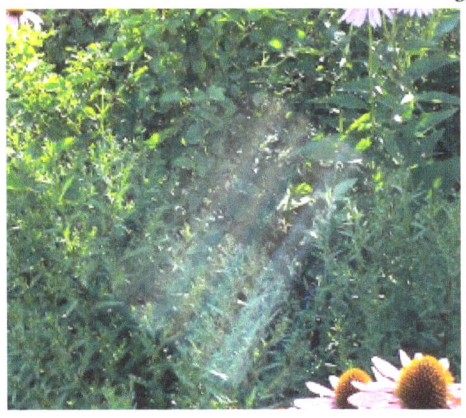

A rare rectangular light being. This is the first and only shot I've taken of one of these.

I used to think my pictures of Orbs were some of the best I'd ever seen. That was until I met Grace Butler online. I found her YouTube channel (Grace Butler) with her pictures and videos shortly before I was ready to publish. I was amazed at her pictures and impressed with her spiritual knowledge. It was not an accident that we found each other. I believe there are no accidents. This book would not be complete without including her spectacular photos and reference to her videos. I save most of her pictures and story for last, because they are so colorful, unique and beautiful.

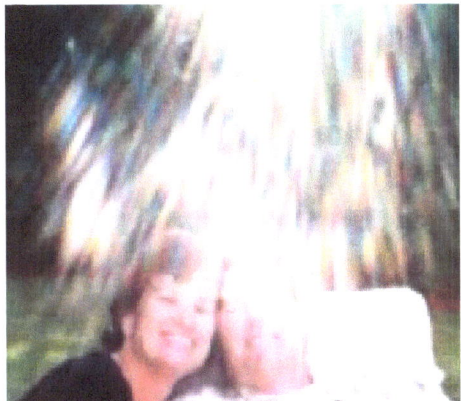

This Rainbow Light Being color burst is becoming more common. A friend let me use this picture. The Light seems to confirm they are a very happy couple.

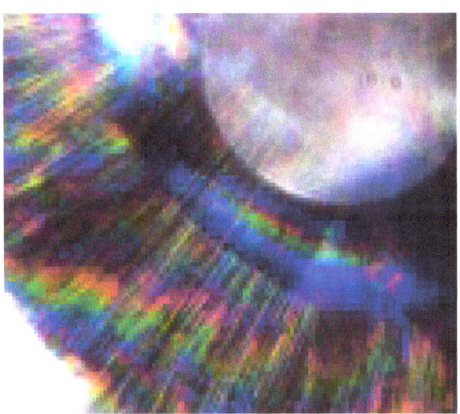

Grace Butler took this amazingly colorful picture of a Rainbow Light Being bursting with color. These two pictures of color bursts look very similar.

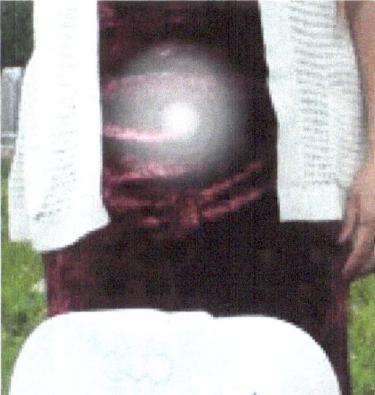

An Orb appears at the gravesite of the "soiled dove" Pearl de Vere in the Mt. Pisgah cemetary near Cripple Creek, Colorado.

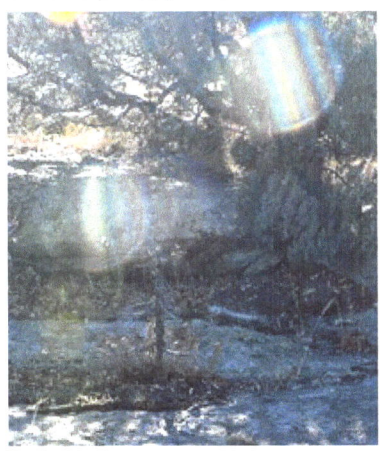

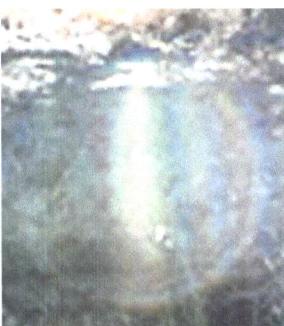

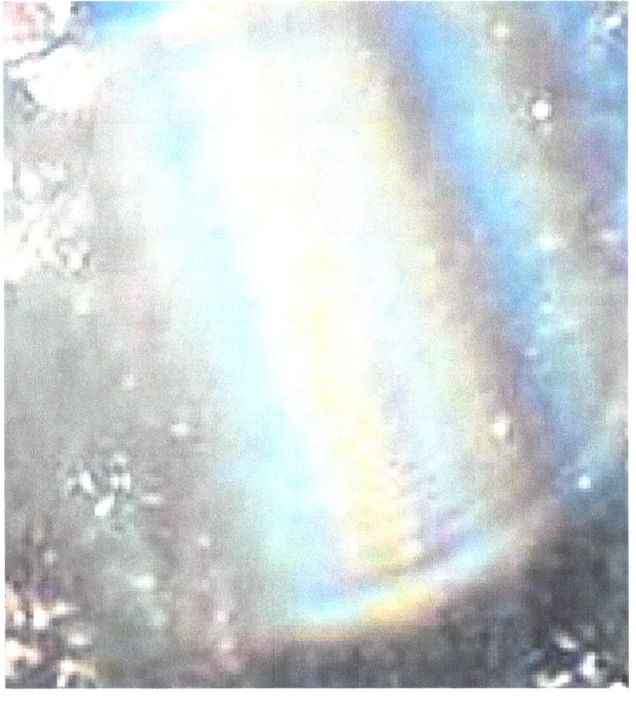

Striped Rainbow Light Being Orb shots taken at Castlewood Canyon, Colorado, 2017. These are the clearest and most colorful orb shots I'd ever taken up until that time. I believe the energy from the rock formations increased their intensity. My main intension for visiting the canyon was to photograph the rock formations, taking as many pictures as possible, in hopes that Orbs would appear. I was delighted to discover, when I reviewed the pictures, that these lovely Light Beings had joined me. The colorful stripes are unusual in my pictures but seem common in those Grace takes.

Luke 11:34 The light of the body is the eye: therefore when thine eye is clear, thy whole body is full of Light.

Light Speed

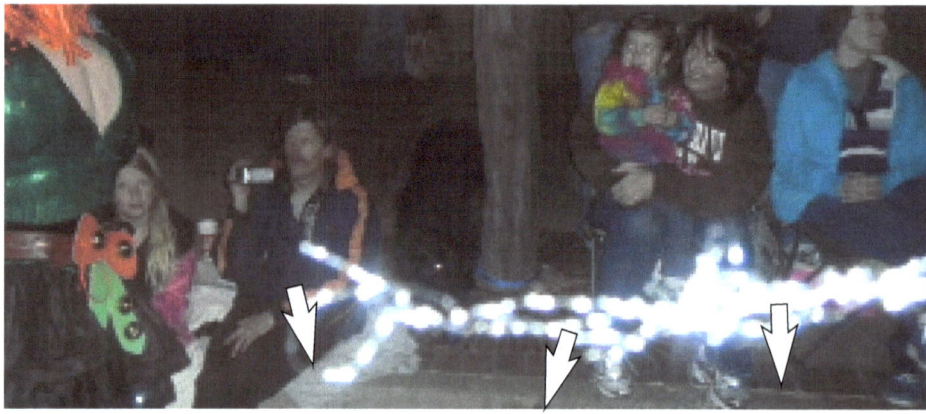 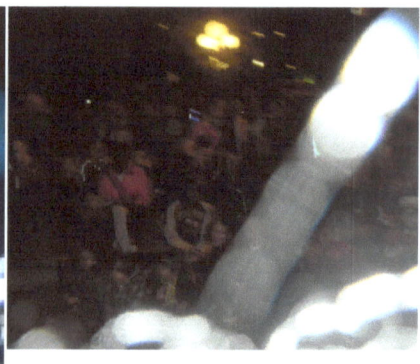

Fast Bouncing Orbs

I think these pictures of Orbs bouncing may be pictures of a single Orb in action moving rapidly. The Light Being behind chasing me in the parade must have been moving with incredible speed. How is this anomaly explained? Were there multiple Light Beings there or was it just one? I'm astonished that this fast movement was captured in the time it takes for a digital camera to take a picture.

The energy of the parade was very high and when I play Jingles I get extremely positive reaction from the crowd. The photographer was my best friend. He joined me in the parade as Jangles the elf. We were both having an absolute blast. Perhaps the combined celebration energy attracted the Light Beings. Maybe orbs show up, not only as an extension of the photographer, but possibly an extension of subject as well. Maybe it's both, either, or neither. In time, conceivably, that question may be answered. Jangles also took the picture of large fast bouncing Orbs during the parade. This is another example of the remarkably high speeds that these Light Beings are capable of. **Can they move at the speed of thought?**

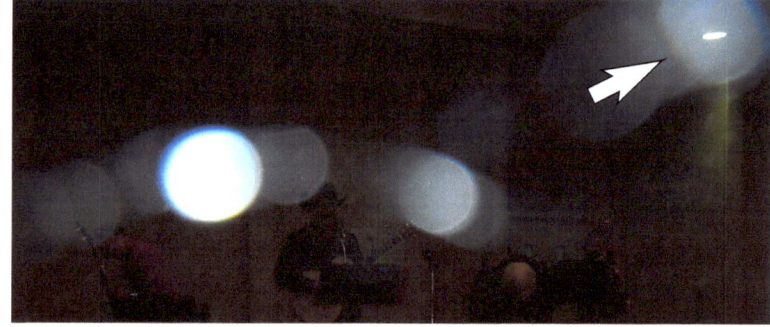

Bouncing Orbs appear at a charity benefit for children with cancer at Christmas. Notice the rod inside the orb at the top right of the picture.

"In some cases there are concentrations of subtle energy outside the camera, in the form of apparitions or Orbs, for example. In the right lighting conditions, these can appear on film. In addition, there may be a high concentration of subtle energy, which has collected inside the camera, either from the environment or the operator. This will bend the light after it enters the camera. (Swanson, 2011)

"It appears that subtle energy phenomena do not always show up in photographs, even when they are witnessed by many people. There is either a subjective aspect to them, or else their appearance depends in some way on the state of the individual at the time of the event." (Life Force, 2011)

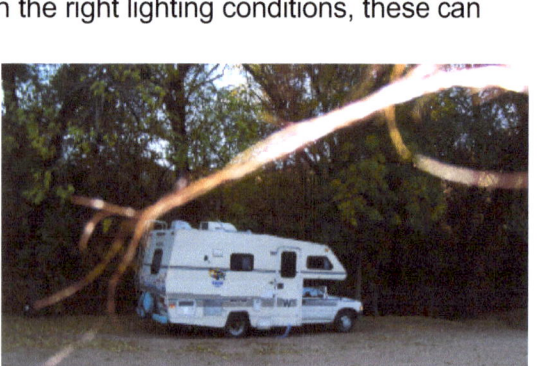

Fast Light Beings appear with my camper. They resemble those chasing me at the parade above.

"Spirit emanations can rapidly expand and contract..."Many images of orbs show them in fast motion, with velocities calculated at over 500 miles per hour, and at possibly even much higher speeds. But airborne particles do not move that fast." (Heinemann, Ph.D., 2010)

Dr. Swanson discusses the "Newton spectrum," in his book, *LIFE FORCE*, which is the normal angle at which light is expected to bend passing through a prism. Dr. Swanson notes that Dr. William Tiller has done experiments where light beams are seen bending the normal amount. At the same time there were **light beams bent at different angles** which are not predicted or expected for normal light. "When Tiller analyzed this strange light, he concluded that it could only occur if some of the light passing through the prism traveled faster than normal light. In other words, some of the light beams acted … **as if they were passing through the prism going faster than the normal speed of light**". (Swanson, 2011) (Emphasis by Swanson) The normal speed of light is 186,282 miles or 299,792 kilometers per second. How fast is Living Light?

"Since the speed of light in air is very close to the speed of light in a vacuum, and is supposed to be the highest speed anything can travel, it is disturbing to learn that the speed of this 'special light' (Living Light?), in the prism, goes 'faster than light'. It appears to be breaking a basic law of physics. This suggests that subtle energy, or the light produced by subtle energy, may travel **faster** than the speed of light in a vacuum. This suggests that the light created by subtle energy may have some truly revolutionary properties." (Swanson, 2011) (Emphasis by Swanson)

"It is conceivable that some advanced race in far stellar reaches has such a profound science that it can manipulate natural forces in a way that allows its members to transfer themselves into other places in the universe that would be unreachable by linear travel, however fast that might be". (Devereux, 1989)

Light Beings are attracted to caves and rock formations. The Piezoelectric Effect may explain this. The Piezoelectric Effect is the ability of certain materials to generate an electrical charge in response to applied mechanical stress. They may be attracted to the crystalline structure of the rocks themselves. Crystals generate subtle energy.

"You've probably used piezoelectricity quite a few times today. If you've got a quartz watch, piezoelectricity is what helps it keep regular time. If you've been writing a letter or an essay on your computer with the help of voice recognition software, the microphone you spoke into probably used piezoelectricity to turn the sound energy in your voice into electrical signals your computer could interpret. If you were a bit of an audiophile and like listening to music on vinyl, your gramophone would have been using piezoelectricity to "read" the sounds from your Long Play records. Piezoelectricity (literally, "pressing electricity") is much simpler than it sounds: it just means using crystals to convert mechanical energy into electricity or vice-versa." (Woodford, 2017)

"Another plausible explanation for some UFO (Light Being) sightings is given in the term "earth lights." It was coined by the English researcher Paul Devereux in his 1982 book of that title and amplified in his 1989 book *Earth Lights Revelations*. His books present evidence that geophysical activity in crystalline rock structures, especially along fault lines, produces piezoelectric effect. That subsurface pressure generates electromagnetic fields above the fault lines, and in those fields, luminous atmospheric phenomena occur. Those luminous atmospheric phenomena are 'earth' lights. Aerial luminosities have been noted throughout history around the world." (White, 1996)

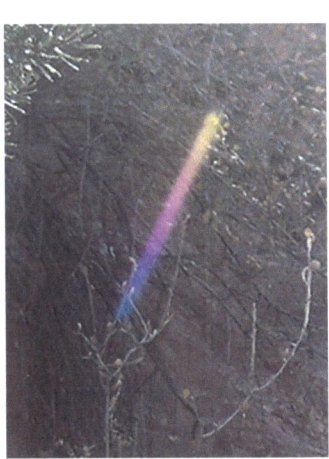

This bright neon rod was one of the first Light Beings to show up and display such vivid colors. Taken in front of a large rock formation, it supports my theory that Light Beings are attracted to rocks and caves. The original picture to the right has another interesting Light Being at the bottom middle of the shot.

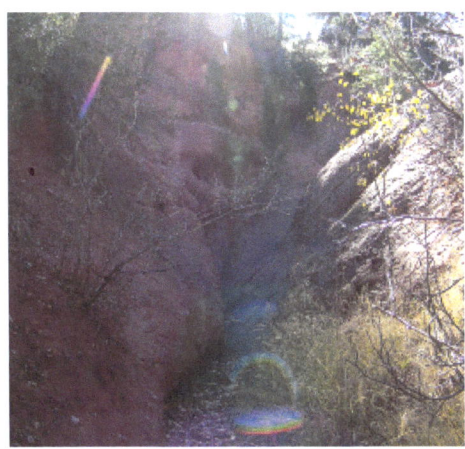

"
There are several other known examples of light phenomena being reported at megalithic sites in Britain, and Norse traditions even had special names for lights associated with stone structure sites ... Geology is thus the gateway into the geophysical arena in which earth lights appear and perform. The geological and seismic connection with terrain related lights is of crucial importance, for it represents a true starting point for their study. It makes possible the opening of a genuine field of research for their study." (Devereux, 1989)

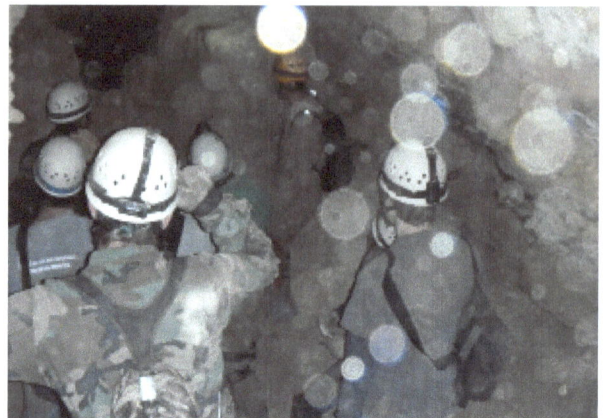

These amazing shots of multiple Orbs were taken while inside the lower levels of the Cave Of The Winds, Manitou Springs, Colorado. All 275 pictures I took during this expedition contained multiple Orbs of different sizes and shapes. These pictures were taken with a digital camera with a flash. What do you think these orbs represent? Why do you think they appeared in my photos?

This is a closeup from one of my caving trip photographs. The dark rim around it's exterior and the brighter white rim are part of this Light Being, as well as its interior. The interior has something that looks alive in it, at least to my eyes. Dust in photos NEVER looks like this.

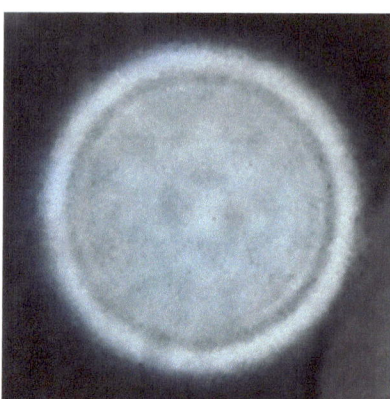

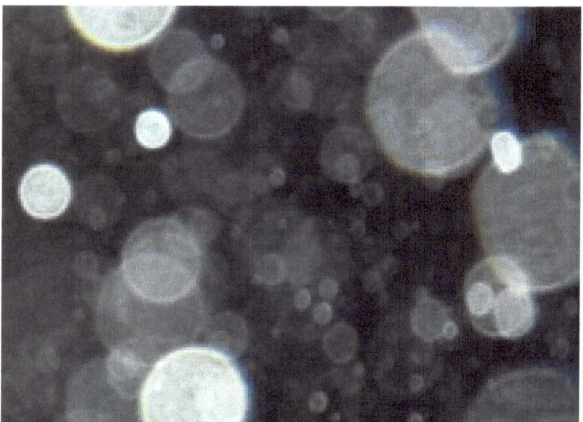

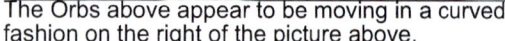

The Orbs above appear to be moving in a curved fashion on the right of the picture above.

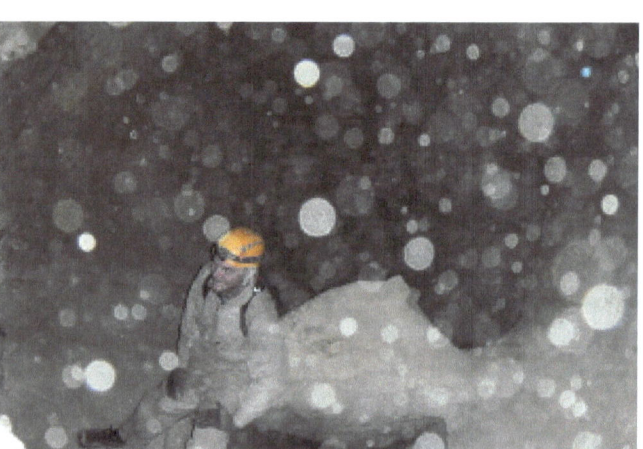

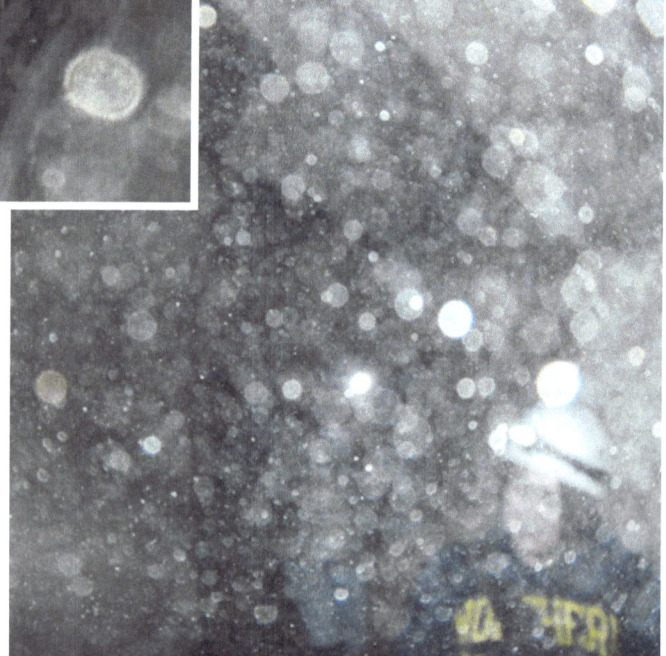

Proverbs 6:23 The law is Light.

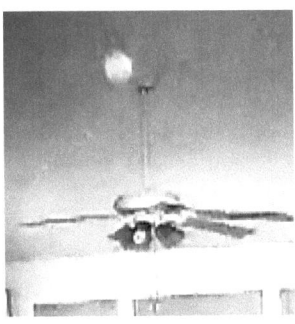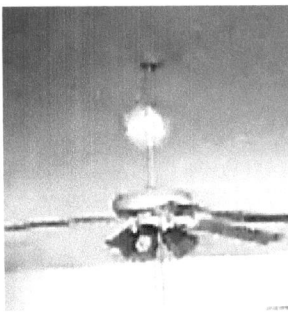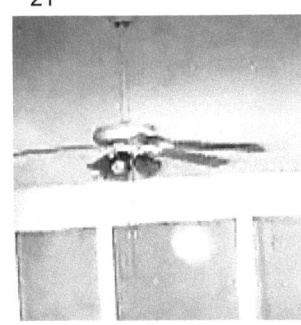

The top three pictures show the movement of an Orb in my house. The orb flys in front of the fan on it's way across the room. The second set of four pictures shows an Orb flying from the door knob to the top corner of the door. These pictures are from the security camera in my living room.

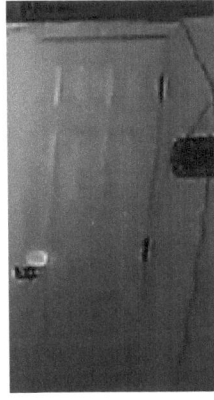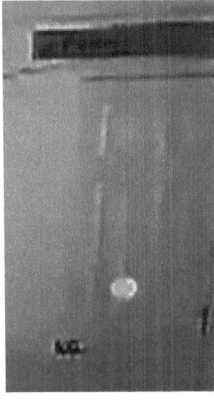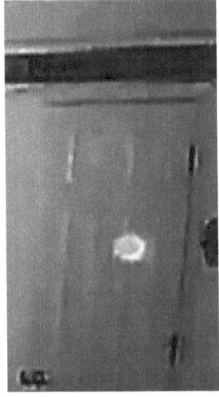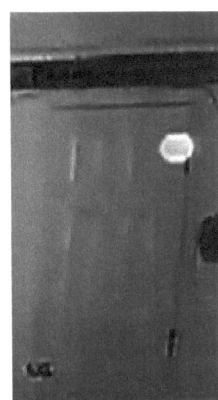

My cameras are inside and outside my house. Light Beings appear more on my outside cameras because they are in infrared mode at night. The inside cameras have more light, so they are not recording in infrared mode at night and fewer Light Beings appear. They show up best when it is dark and the cameras are in infrared mode. My cameras automatically switch to infrared mode when it gets dark. They also show up when the security cameras are recording in broad daylight.

I see Orbs every day on my security cameras and in YouTube videos. Sometimes no orbs appear on any of my eight cameras. When I invite them in they appear on multiple cameras within moments. I think they are responding to my desire to see them.

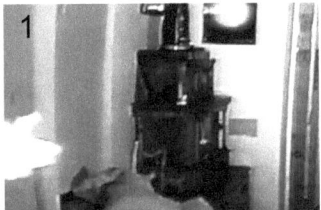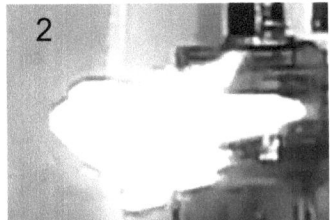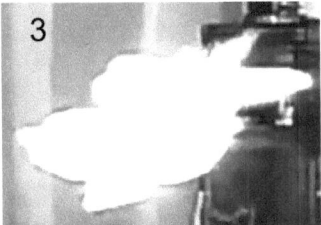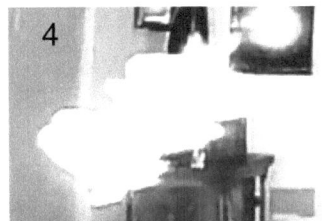

This Light Being changes shape as it propels itself. These different "configurations" are of the same object. The Light Being appears at the bottom left of the screen. The first picture shows the size of the original object and the piece of furniture across the room from it. All the following shots have been cropped. The first picture puts the size of the object into perspective. It increased in size as it moved. All other pictures have been zoomed and cropped to show the changes in greater detail. If you use the dark piece of furniture behind the Light Being as a focus, it's easy to track its forward progress. It starts out with what looks like wings. As it moved toward the furniture it changed shape as it moved. It looks like it's jumping or stretching as it moves forward. It's shape changed as it changed itself from a simple shape to a shape that looks like multiple Light Beings. It seemed to stretch and then reform itself as it moved. Then it lost all shape, and turned into a bright light that fills the picture. After becoming a shapeless bright light, the object reforms itself into what looks like a single entity. After "collecting itself," it resembles a flying bird or angel. The Light Being then flies out of camera range.

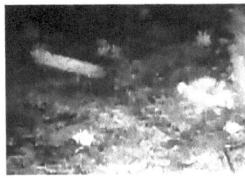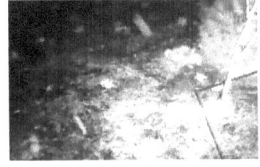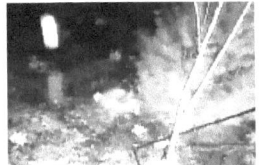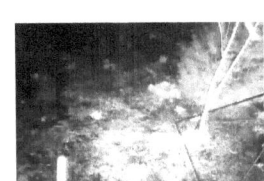

These pictures came from one of my security cameras shower". It was not raining, snowing and there were watched this phenomenon live on my security monit The Orbs and rod Light Beings were swarming in the video. They moved in all different directions. There were too many to count, and because they were moving so fast, it was difficult to get clear still shots from what I recorded. These pictures show movement and variety. It looks like it's snowing or raining, and without my discription of what I was witnessing, anyone looking at these pictures might assume that this was a weather event. An Orb shower can be seen in *Living Light* - The *Documentary* on YouTube around a bridge on the Hindenburg line in France. The Orb shower is inside the tunnel and all around it. Countless men perished during the war in the tunnel. The Light Beings may be attracted to the energy remaining in the area. The Light Beings may be the souls, or spirits, of those who died there.

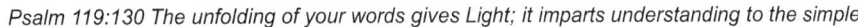

Psalm 119:130 The unfolding of your words gives Light; it imparts understanding to the simple.

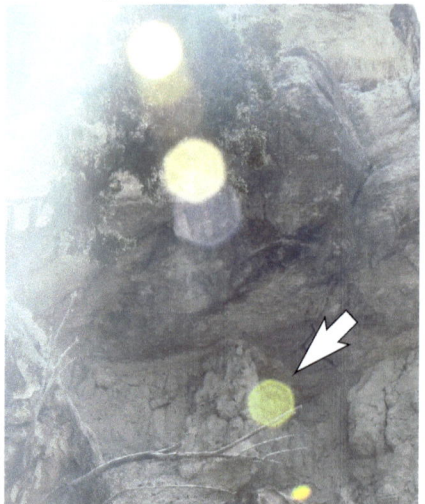

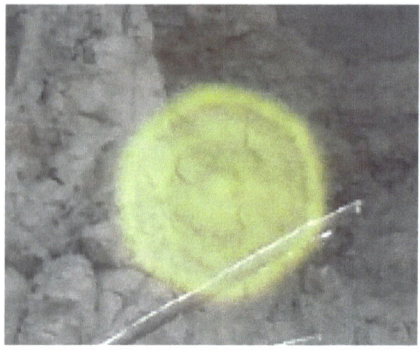

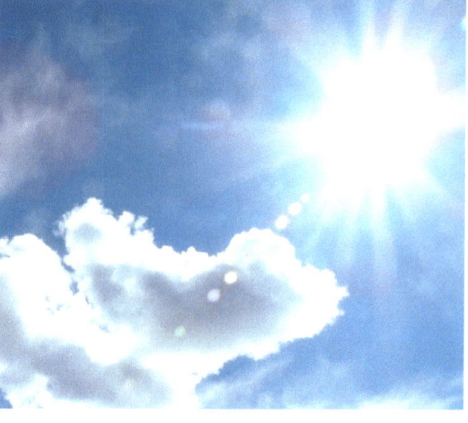

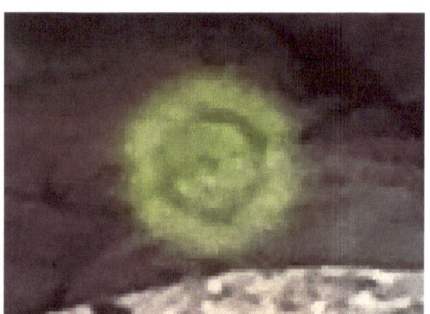

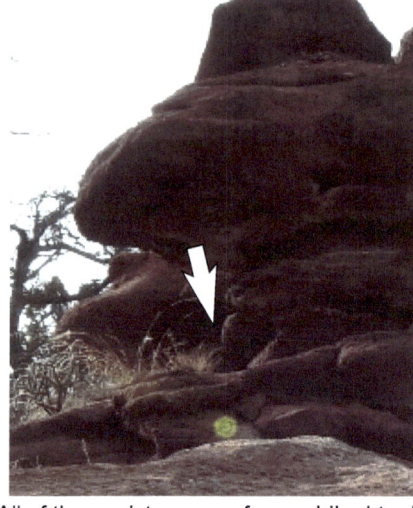

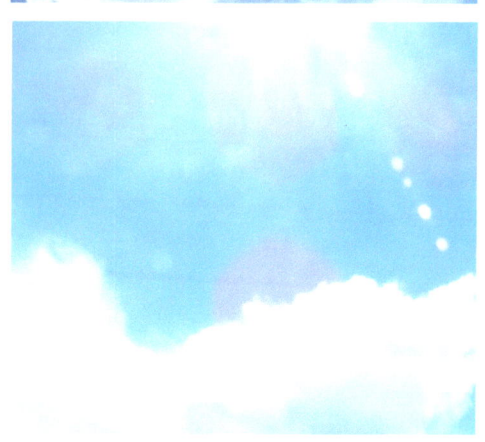

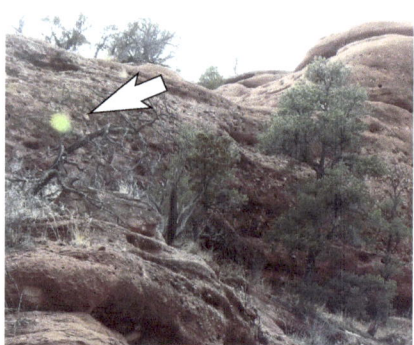

All of these pictures are from a hike I took in March 2018. I used to think that the colorful shapes in sunbeams were just refraction, so I haven't been paying much attention to them. Now I realize that the sunbeam shapes are actually Light Beings that show up because the sun illuminates them at a certain angle. The reason I believe this now is because of these pictures. The sunbeam shot with the green enlarged Orb taken from the beam is the same shape and color as the singular Orb of the same shape and color that appears singularly. Furthermore, the sunbeams in the sky are surrounded by pale Light Beings that aren't in the sunbeams. These pictures were taken an hour apart and 74 pictures apart. I had been wondering about the sunbeam/refraction question for quite some time. The Orbs decided it was time to answer my unspoken question so that I would know beyond a shadow of a doubt. I will be looking for more examples to prove my theory in future pictures that I take and movies that I watch. It's a game of "I Spy", and I enjoy playing it! Where's WaldOrb?

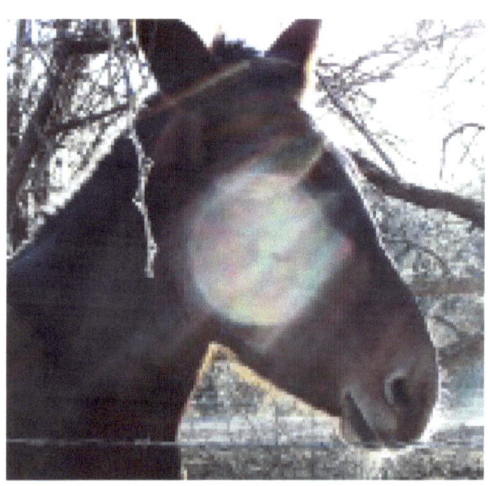

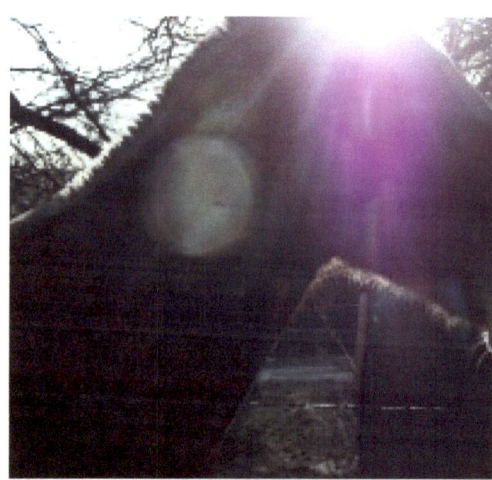

Light Beings appear near animals. My cats play with things that aren't there. They get up on their back legs and bat at what appears to be nothing. Since whatever they are playing with is invisible to my eye, I believe they are playing with Light Beings. Since cats can see at night, it means that they see different spectrums of light. Perhaps they can see like an infrared camera sees. Grace took these pictures of a mule with Light Beings with no flash.

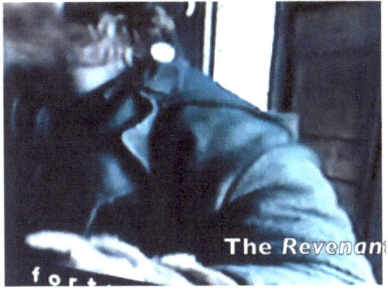

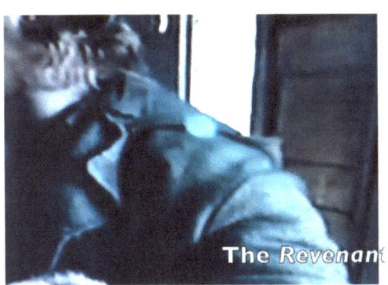

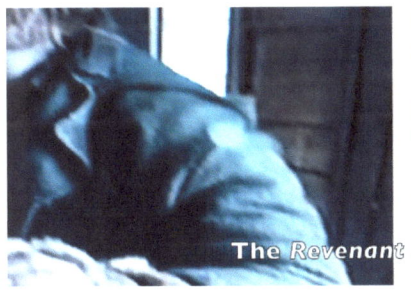

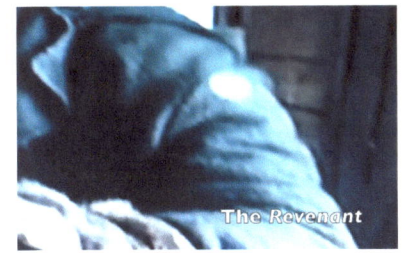

I am very familiar with moving Orbs caught on security cameras. The fact that they record a different spectrum of light is the reason more show up under infared. I had no idea how many moving Light Beings appear in old and new motion pictures and videos. I had never noticed them before.

My son took me to see the movie *"The Revenant"* in the theater. I was enjoying the movie, when to my surprise, a brite white orb appears out of an actors shoulder and moved down his arm. I was thrilled! To see an Orb in a theater filmed with a movie camera was exciting! What else had I missed?

I waited for the movie to come out on DVD. I remembered the exact scene and found it easily on the DVD. Sure enough, there was the Orb, plain as day. I played it on my TV and filmed it with my cell phone. I have included it in my documentary, *"Living Light – The Documentary"* on YouTube. The documentary shows the Orb in motion. These shots taken from that footage, illustrate the same phenomenon. My eyes seem to have been opened by this experience, and ever since I see orbs in almost every movie, documentary or video I watch. I see them almost daily in the tarot readings I watch on YouTube. Recently I was watching one and the reader reaches for a tarot card and says "come to mama". As soon as she said that a small bright Light Being appeared behind her and headed straight for her, blinking, stopping, changing direction and clearly making it's presence known. This appeared to be a deliberate communication. I could be wrong.

Light Beings are Intelligent and may have cognitive and psychic abilities they've developed so that they can show up in pictures and movies.

- Did they know ahead of time that people would notice and expose them?
- Did they know their existence would be noticed, because of our improved technology?
- Are they helping lift the veil so we can see into other dimensions?
- Do they know that by expanding humanities understanding of this phenomenon, paradigms may shift?

Perceptions of reality may be expanded by this phenomenon. Those receptive to open-minded educational information will benefit. Could Light Beings be sending inspirational messages telepathically to everyone now?

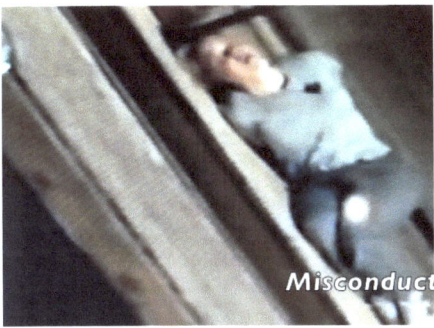

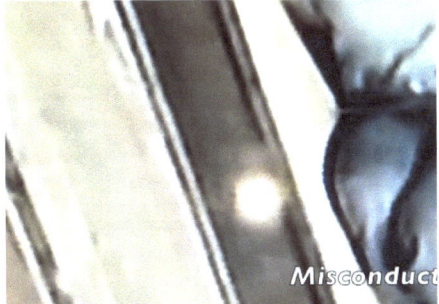

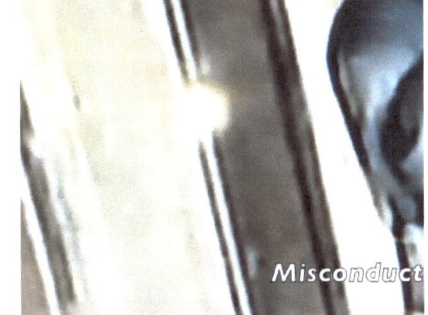

A clear bright round orb is seen here in the movie *Misconduct*. Watch the movie and see if you can find this scene. Now that you know what to look for, I bet you'll spot it. It's like playing a game of Where's Waldo. I search for Light Beings in every movie I watch now. I keep my eyes peeled and look for them. I usually find them.

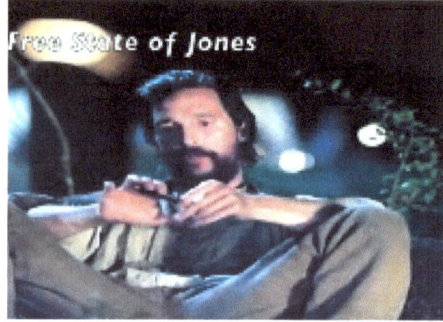

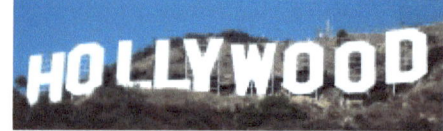

A bright yellow fast moving Light Being moves directly in front of Matthew McConaugheys' face in the recent movie "*Free State of Jones*". As I watch older movies and see Light Beings in them, I realize Light Beings have been in movies all along.

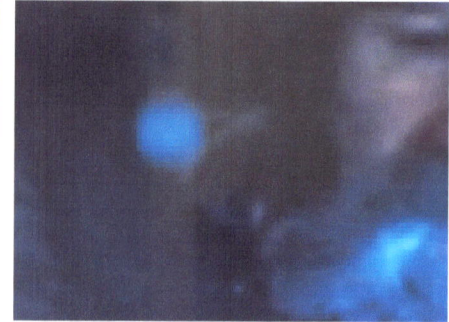

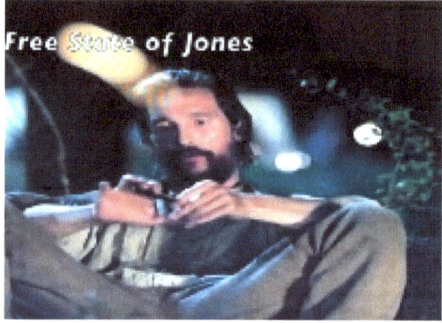

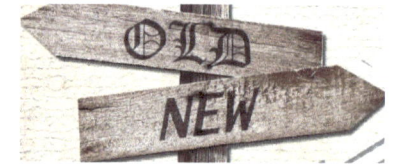

These shape shifting Light Beings fly beside Julia Roberts, in the movie "*I Love Trouble*". They are not bugs or dust on the lense. What are they and why are they there?

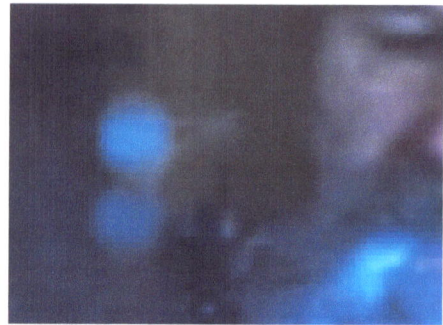

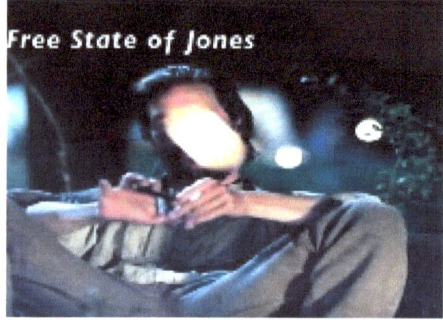

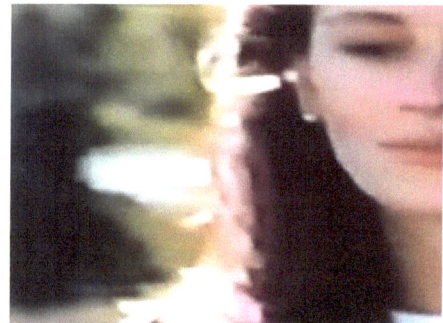

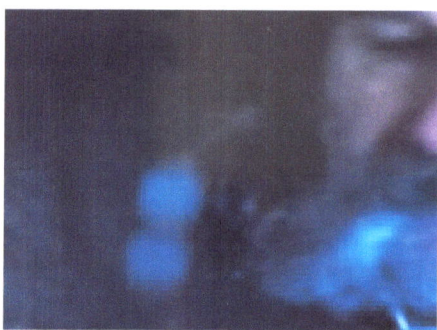

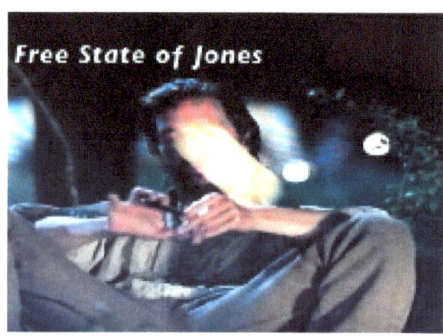

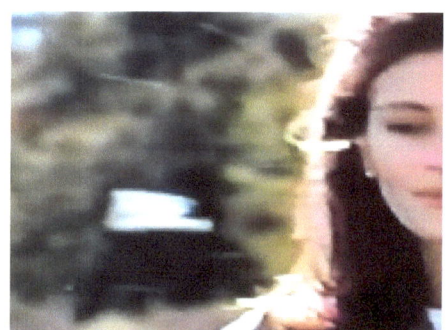

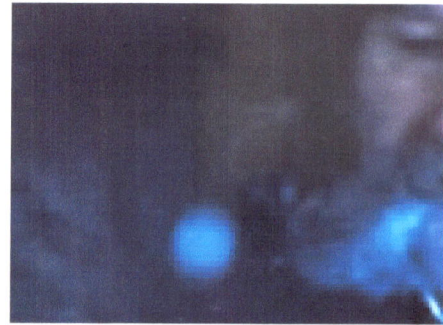

Large blue Orbs appear with Kurt Russell in the movie *The Hateful Eight*. Watch the stagecoach scene in the movie where Russell is reading a letter from President Lincoln. You'll see the blue Orbs moving beside him if you pay close attention.

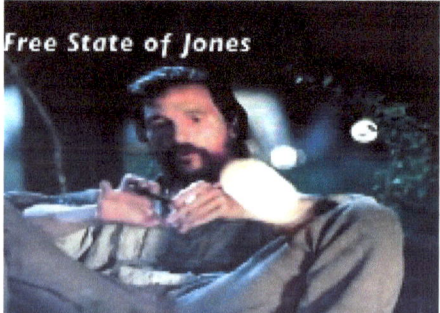

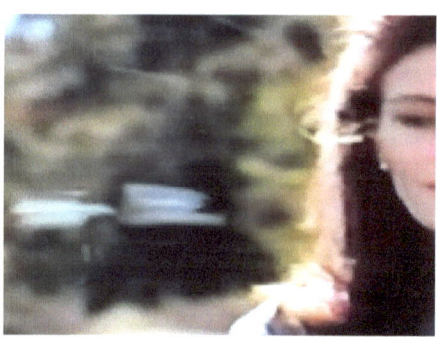

1 Thessalonians 5:5 Ye are all children of he light and the children of the day.

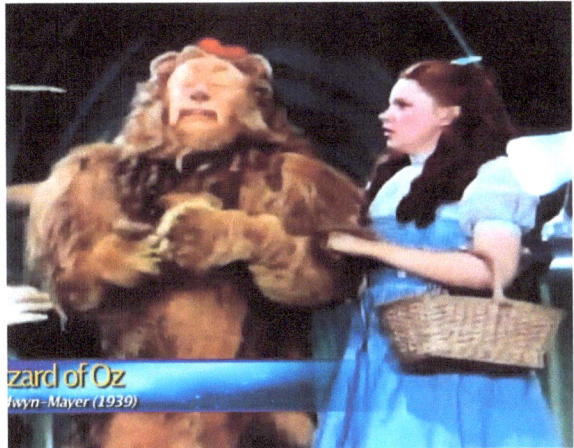

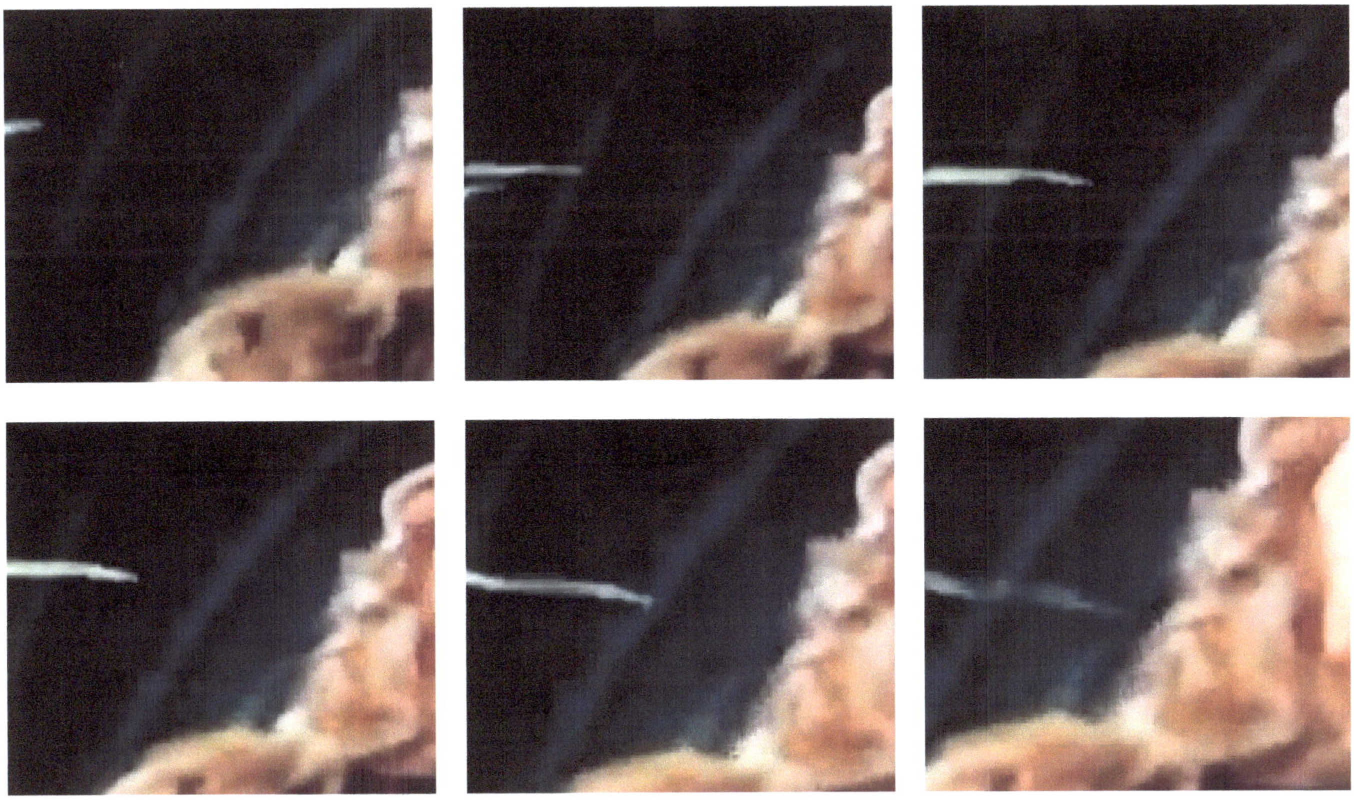

This Light Being starred in *The Wizard of Oz,* one of the most popular movies of all time. It shape shifts as it moves across the screen. When I first saw this Light Being, I thought it was a piece of straw from the Scare Crow. These are examples of its movement as seen in movie. *The Wizard of Oz* was filmed using three four hundred pound Technicolor cameras. Each camera recorded a different color: red, green and blue. These images where then combined to create the movie. The fact that this Light Being was recorded by all three cameras and merged into the movie defies explanation.

I find it interesting that the beginning of the Wizard of Oz was filmed in black and white. When Dorothy opens the door, after she is taken by a tornado over the rainbow, everything has color. She finds herself in an alternate reality. The earliest Orb pictures I took had no color. They appeared as white or shades of grey. Grace Butler reports the same lack of color in her earlier Orb pictures.

I believe Dorothys' journey to Oz was a journey into another dimension, if only in her dreams. As we lift our consciousness we begin to glimpse other dimensions. Perhaps that's why the more recent Orb pictures are becoming more colorful. As we see into other dimensions more is revealed.

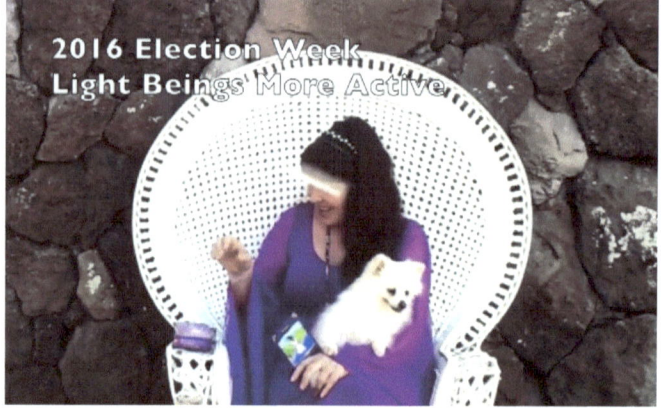

2016 Election Week
Light Beings More Active

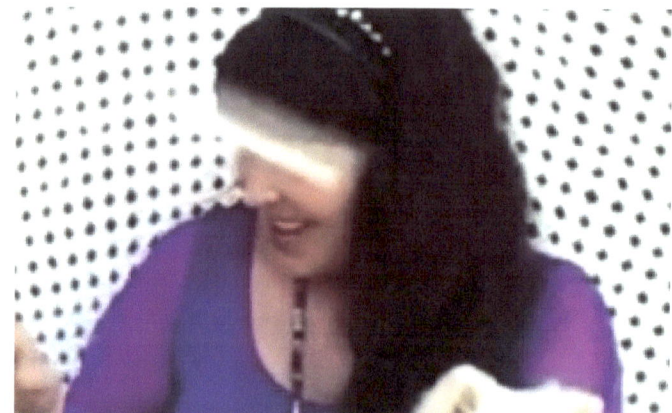

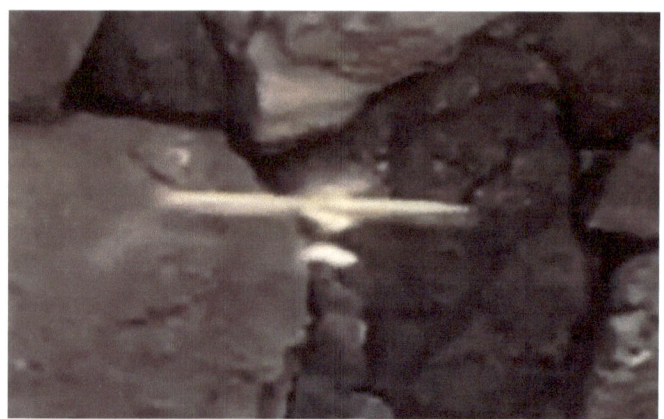

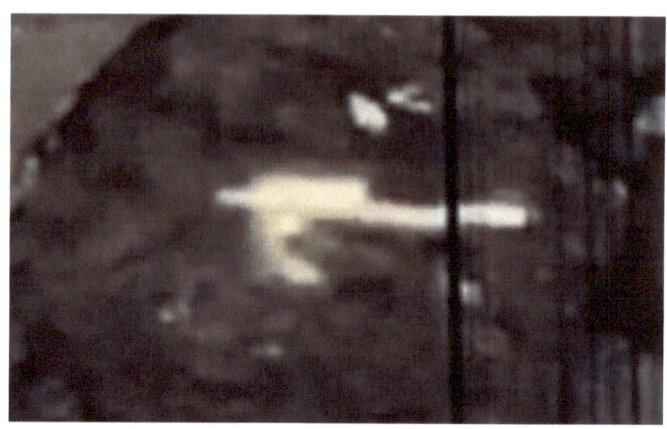

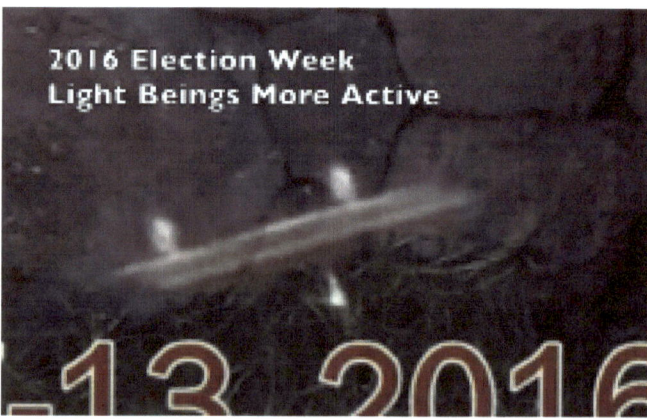

2016 Election Week
Light Beings More Active

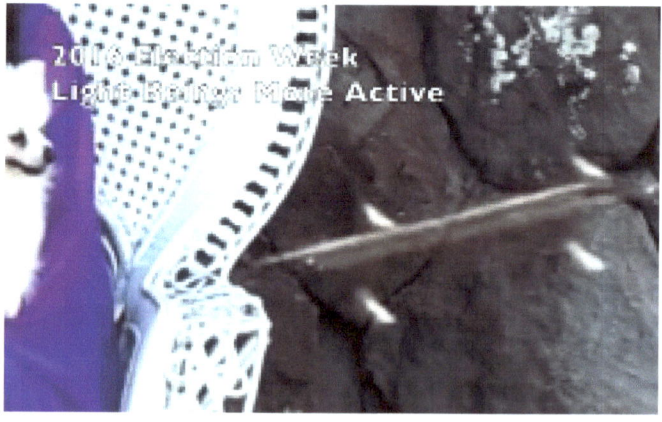

2016 Election Week
Light Beings More Active

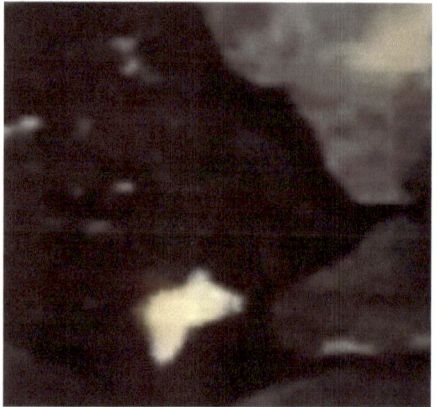

The video these shots came from was filmed on the day of the US Presidential election, 7/13/2016. I think the Light Beings showed up to express themselves because of the focused energy that was vibrating that day. I'd never captured such a variety of shape and movement before. The bright white Light Beings covering Doreen's eyes is referred to as a rod. The Light Beings at the bottom of the page appear to have fins. This type of Light Being has been called an "air fish". As the Light Beings flew from one side of the screen to the other, the number of "fins" changed. What does this fin number change mean? Is this an example of "bioenergetic propulsion?" Do they use their "fins" to fly? The butterfly shaped Light Beings to the left reminds me of the dove Light Being that flew through my house and was caught on camera. These pictures were taken from one of Doreen Virtues' YouTube angel card readings.

Allah is the Light of the heavens and the earth.
(35th verse of the 24th Sura of the Quran, Sura an-Nu)

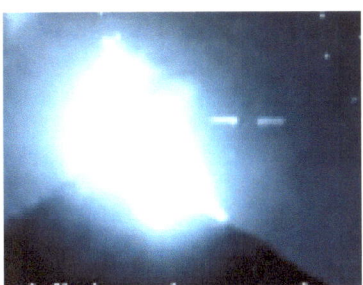

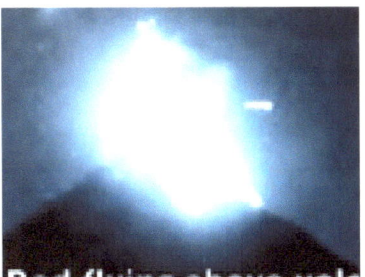

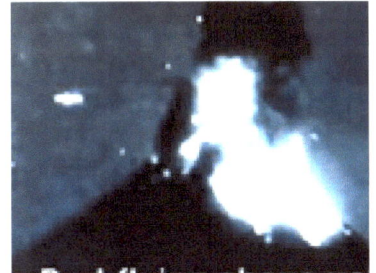

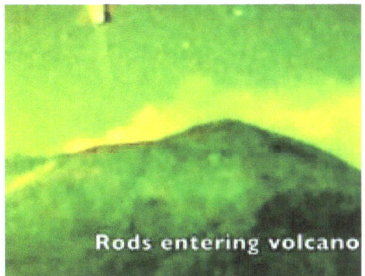

Rods entering volcano

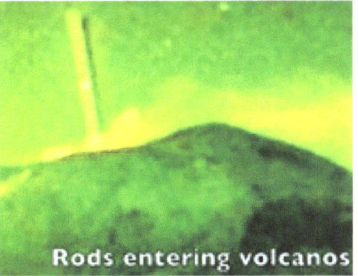

Rods entering volcanos

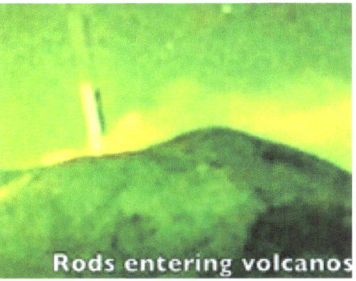

Rods entering volcanos

Light Beings seem to be concerned about natural disasters and show up when they are in progress. Orbs are visible in news footage of the Tsunami in Thailand, 2004. They appear at volcanic eruptions, tornados and during thunderstorms.

"Geophysicists have investigated this phenomenon for a long time because of reports during earthquake activity that the shaking earth was accompanied by aerial lights. The lights weren't called UFOs, of course – just-strange luminosities that sometimes appeared in association with earthquakes. In the mid-1980's, the U.S. Geological Survey, in its journal *Earthquakes and Volcanoes*, published the first photo of one ever; someone with enough presence of mind, to shoot it during an earthquake here in the U.S, snapped it. A vaguely defined ball of light was clearly visible in the air." (Devereux, 1989)

These volcano shots came from two different YouTube videos. They prove that Light Beings do not require a certain atmosphere to exist. Apparently, temperature and volcanic gases do not affect them. According to Devereux, "Mount St Helens erupted 5/18/80. Before the 1980 explosion, researchers were getting reports of unusual lights and anomalous events". (Devereux, 1989)

The jumping rod shaped Light Beings flying through the fire at the top of the volcano illustrate that atmospheric conditions do not affect them.

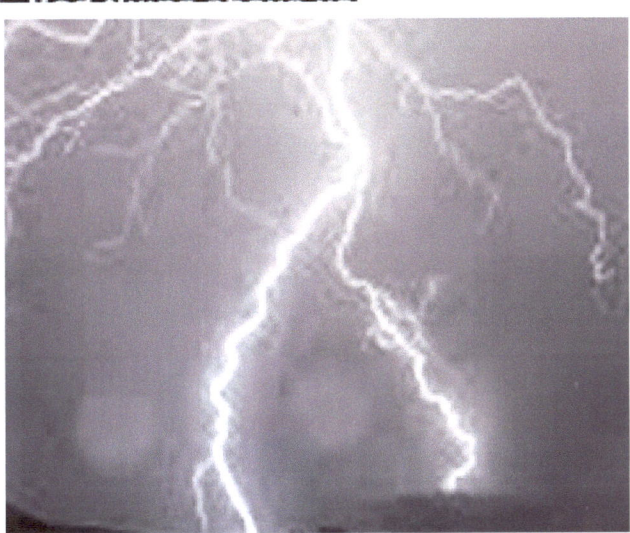

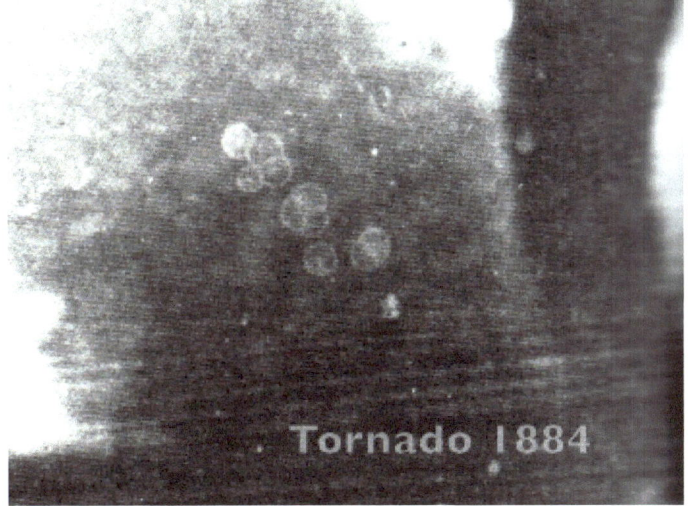

Tornado 1884

Orbs have been witnessed around armed nucular missiles which mysteriously become disarmed. "One of the more out-of-the-ordinary press conferences held in Washington this week consisted of former Air Force personnel testifying to the existence of UFOs (Orbs) and their ability to neutralize American and Russian nuclear missiles." (CBS News 9/28/2010) Light Beings also appear when chemtrails are being sprayed. Chemtrails are the toxic lines disturbing our skies. I've seen videos of orbs that appear to "shoot" something at the chemtrails. Are they attempting to nuetralize the poisons and viruses that are being sprayed on unsuspecting victims globally? Are they attempting to disable the Nanobots the sprays contain? Experts warn that self-replicating Nanobots could destroy all life on Earth. Nanobots are tiny robots only a single nanometer wide (one billionth of a meter) may dominate the planet in the future, if they get out of control. Do Light Beings know all of humanity is being subjected to invisible terrorism, and they are concerned? I am concerned. If you are not concerned perhaps you don't know that it's becoming hazardous to your health to breath.

"If you Light a lamp for somebody, it will also brighten your path." Buddha

The "Tether Incident" took place February 1996, during Space Shuttle Columbia mission STS-75. The primary objective of STS-75 was to carry the Tethered Satellite System Reflight (TSS-1R) into orbit, and to deploy it spaceward on a conducting tether.

NASA wanted to see if they could produce electricity using the tether. According to David Seredas' analysis: "an overload of highly charged particles flooded the tether and produced so much electricity that the tether snapped." The tether broke away from the shuttle and drifted 77 miles away.

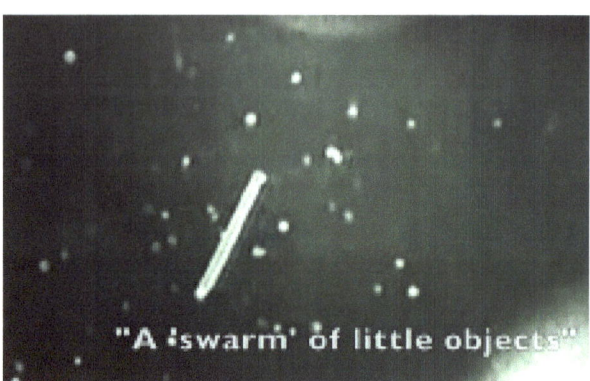

"A 'swarm' of little objects"

A swarm of little balls of light (Orbs or Light Beings) came moving in from all different directions with different velocities around the tether, as seen in the NASA footage. Perhaps NASA was attempting to generate electricity to power space weapons and the Light Beings caused the tether to break to prevent this from happening.

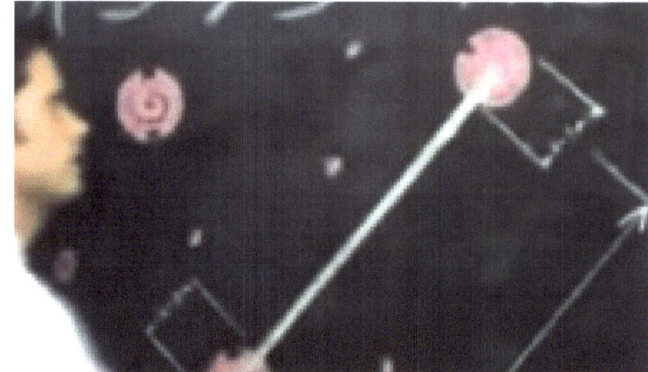

Sereda used the twelve-mile length of the tether as a relative measuring rod for calculating the minimum diameter of some of the discs.

According to his calculations, based on the fact that the objects he was measuring were moving behind the tether, the discs (Orbs) were determined to be **two to three miles wide**.

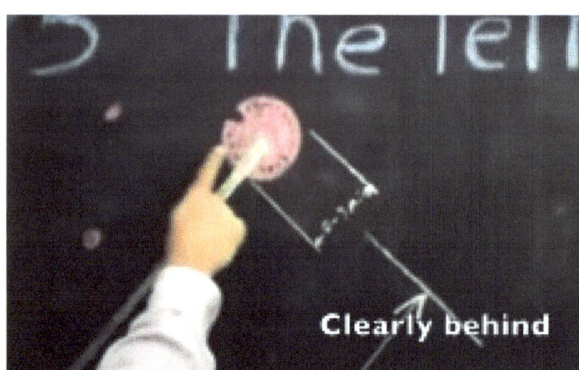

Clearly behind

These diameters are based on the assumption that the objects are right up next to the tether. If they are farther away from the tether, **the discs ()rbs) could be much larger than two to three miles wide.**

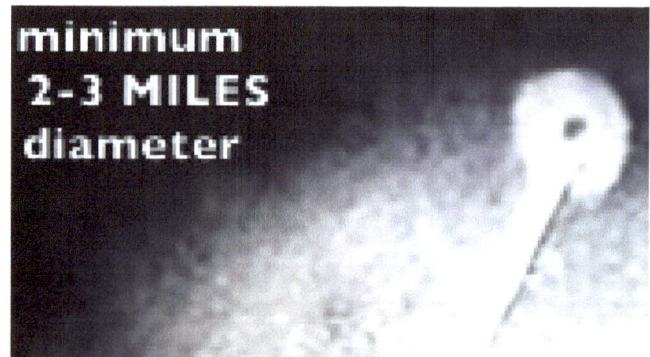

minimum
2-3 MILES
diameter

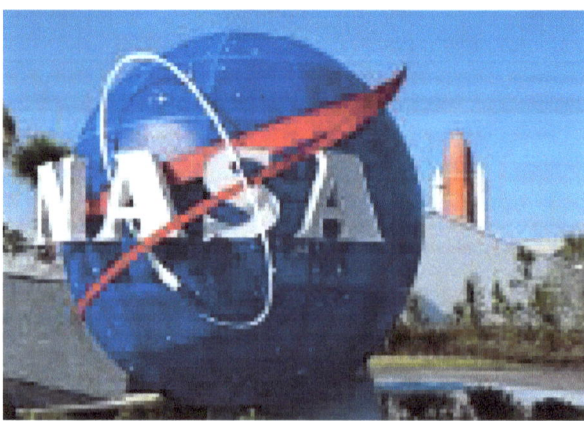

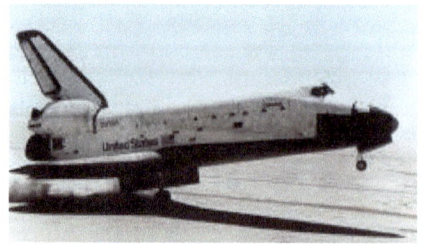

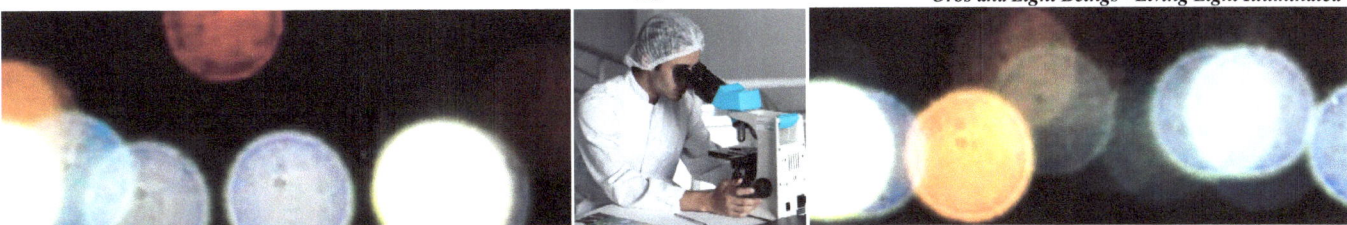

These multicolored orb shots were taken from a YouTube video. The video shows them blinking in and out of the picture. All of the orbs were moving in a forward direction. The cell like appearance of these Light Beings is worth considering. Do they have nuclei? They appear to have a cellular structure.

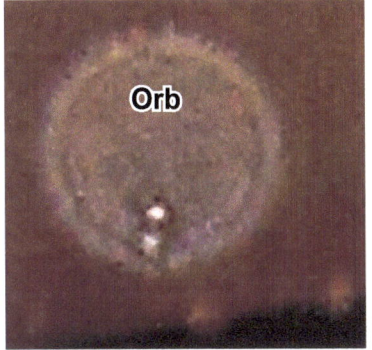

Do Orbs = Cells?
Are they related?

Pictures of orbs to the right and left have an uncanny resemblance to cells under magnification. Is there a connection? Are orbs cells, or are cells orbs in physical form? I find it very interesting that they are so similar.

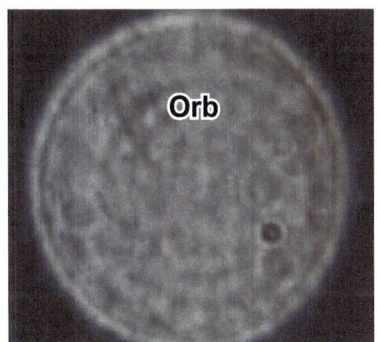

Orb

Orb

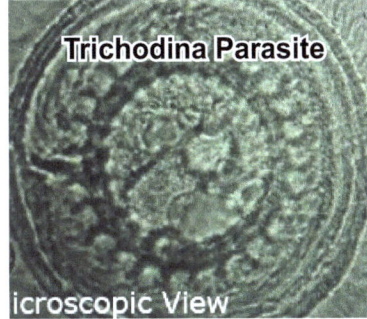

Trichodina Parasite

icroscopic View

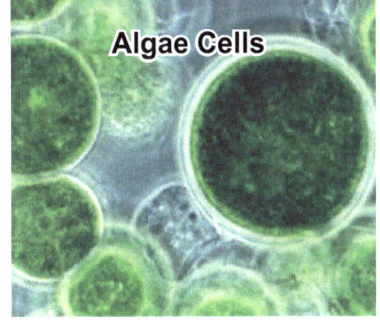

Algae Cells

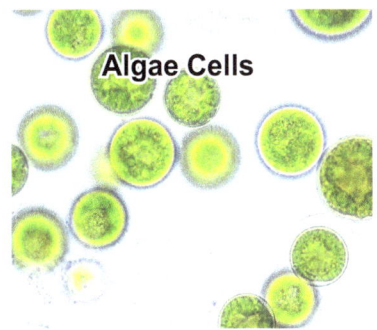

Algae Cells

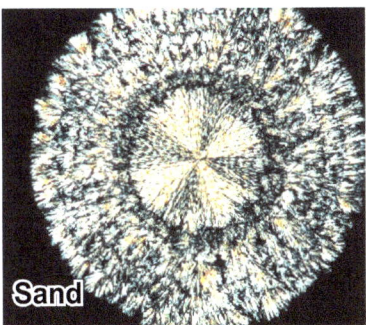

Sand

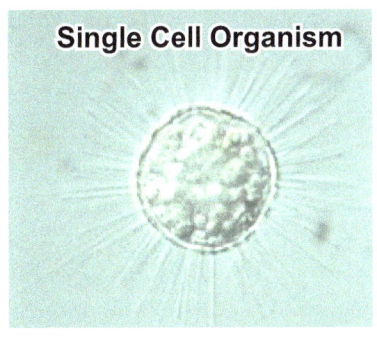

Single Cell Organism

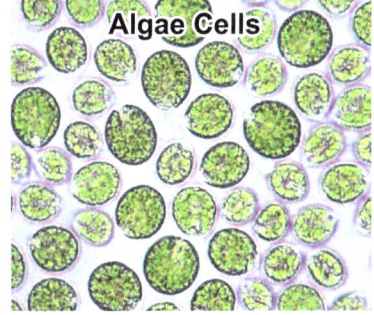

Algae Cells

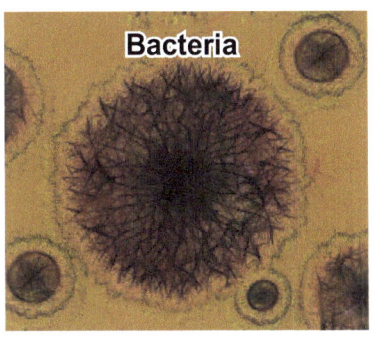

Bacteria

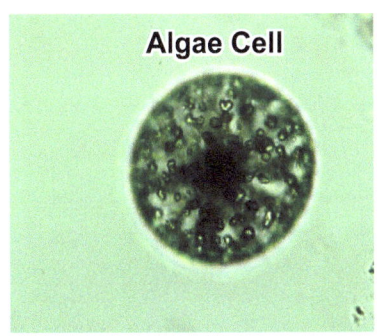

Algae Cell

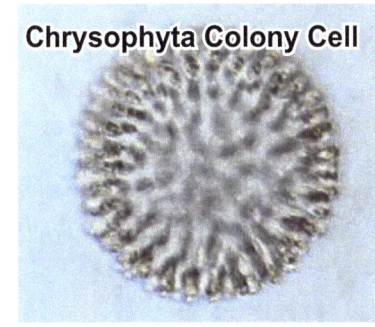

Chrysophyta Colony Cell

"It is during our darkest moments that we must focus to see the Light." Buddha

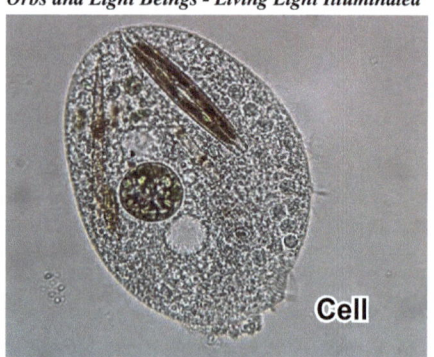

Cell

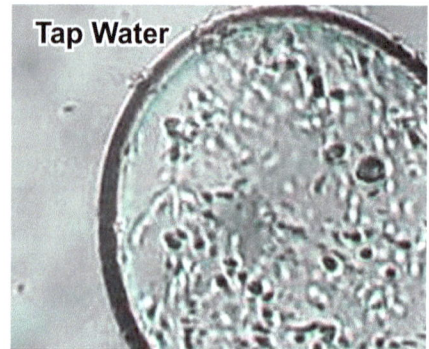

Tap Water

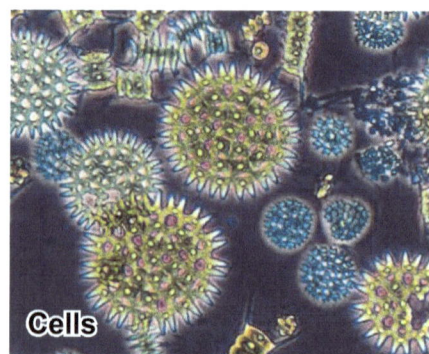

Cells

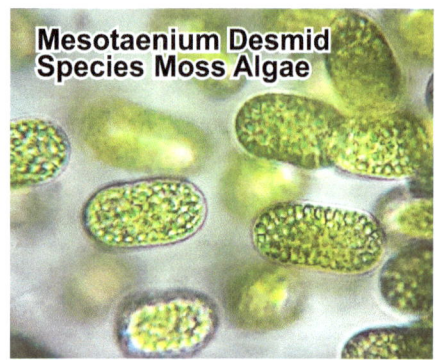

Mesotaenium Desmid Species Moss Algae

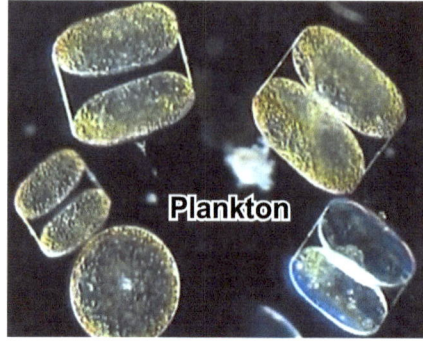

Plankton

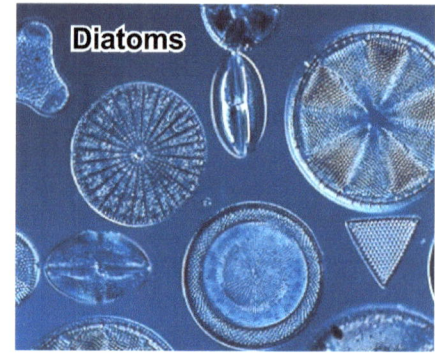

Diatoms

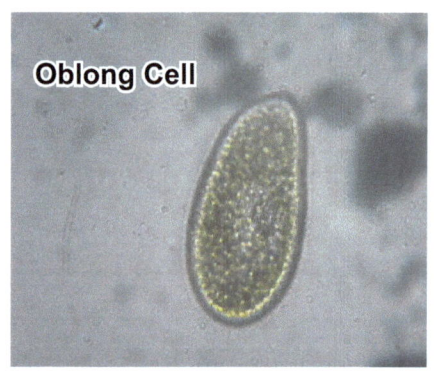

Oblong Cell

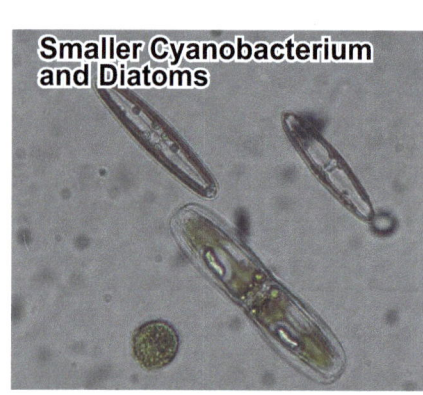

Smaller Cyanobacterium and Diatoms

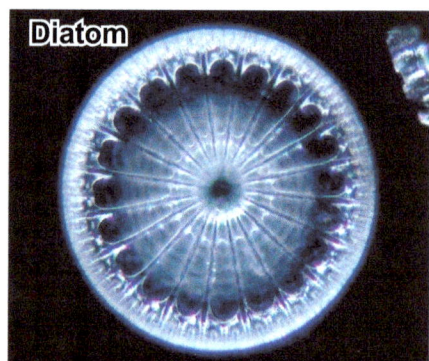

Diatom

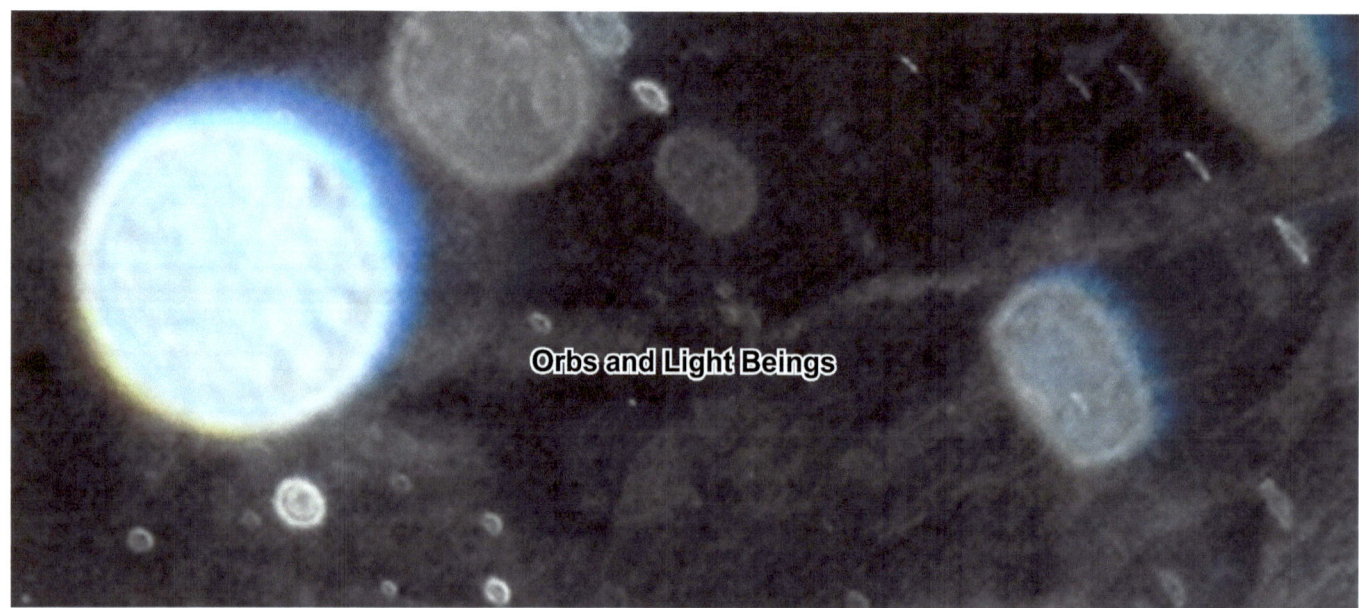

Orbs and Light Beings

"The greatest quality is seeking to serve others." Buddha

Harmonic Convergence is an exceptionally rare planetary alignment, which occurs once every ten thousand years. During Harmonic Convergence of August 16-17, 1987, I participated in a global synchronized meditation event. The purpose of this event was to create a Global signal of synchronized human intention, acting on behalf of a positive future for planet Earth. People everywhere participated as we heralded the dawning of the Age of Aquarius. According to many, when the planets align as they did during Harmonic Convergence, spiritual energy is greatly amplified. This causes the polar spirit portals at the North and South Poles to merge, while an aura of spirit energy envelops the Earth. Many believe the spirits of Light and dark battle for the fate of the world during Harmonic Convergence. Millions of people gathered at sacred sites around the world and joined together to meditate on and vibrate peace, joy, love and Light to ALL. We created a coherent spiritual radio broadcast system, radiating peaceful intensions. Many people reported significant shifts in consciousness and a reorientation in their life patterns after this event.

"The Harmonic Convergence of August 15-16, 1987, was an example of how planetary alignments synchronized with much ancient esoteric wisdom, the Mayan Calendar and the Hopi prophecies in particular. At this time there were seven planets in fire signs, symbolizing the purifying as well as the destructive aspects of the times we are entering." (Earth Mother Astrology: Llewellyn Publications)

Prophecy indicates that the world will be purified by fire. This does not mean a physical burning fire as some have misinterpreted this purification to be. It has to do with the fire energy associated with the planets. When planets align their combined energy is amplified, and this amplified fire energy is burning away the veil of illusion the Piscean age imposed.

The Age of Aquarius is not part of astronomy. It's an astrological age, which occurs because of a real motion of Earth known as the precession of the equinoxes. The Age of Aquarius begins when the March equinox point moves out of the constellation Pisces and into the constellation Aquarius. In other words, the Piscean Age (the Age of Pisces) has ended and the "new age", the Age of Aquarius, has begun.

The Age of Pisces was all about power and control. It could be called the "Age of Deception" because secrets and elitism reigned. Key words defining the Piscean Age include: deception, illusion, hidden, misled, confusion, fear, secrets, false, fake, greed, materialism, separation, addiction, control and domination. The Piscean values of money, power and control are being replaced. They do not resonate with the values of the Age of Aquarius.

The values of the Age of Aquarius are love, community, unity, integrity, freedom, equality and fraternity. The 1967 musical *Hair*, by James Rado and Gerome Ragni, introduced the concept of the Age of Aquarius to the world. The Fifth Dimension, an apropos name for a "new age" musical group, recorded the song, *Aquarius/Let the Sunshine In*. It became a huge hit. The lyrics of this song define the Age of Aquarius for me:

"When the moon is in the Seventh House, and Jupiter aligns with Mars (Harmonic Convergence), then peace will guide the planets, and love will steer the stars. This is the dawning of the Age of Aquarius. Harmony and understanding, sympathy and trust abounding; No more falsehoods or derisions, golden living dreams of visions, mystic crystal revelation, and the mind's true liberation, Aquarius. Let the sunshine; let the sunshine in, the sunshine in." (sunshine = Light)

I had multiple Light Being or UFO sightings during Harmonic Convergence in 1987. I'd gone to Joshua Tree National Monument in California for a sacred ceremony with over one hundred other people. When I arrived at the guard shack I noticed a bright flashing star just above the horizon. This struck me as odd. It was flashing white, yellow, blue, green and red. I asked the guard about the star and she told me it wasn't a star and that it had been in the same location since sunrise. Very interesting. When I got to my campsite I climbed on top of a large rock formation and saw three more flashing lights at the same level above the horizon. Each was at a compass point marking north, south, and east. The light I'd seen originally was to the west. The flashing lights stayed in their positions until after our closing ceremony the following day. Then all four of them disappeared at the same time.

The night before the closing ceremony, I saw a pair of small white lights very high in the sky traveling together in an erratic fashion. They'd do zigzags and loops, then straight lines and slow curves. I wondered if anyone else attending had seen something similar.

"We are what we think. All that we are arises with our thoughts." Buddha

After the closing ceremony, I asked for a show of hands of anyone who had seen anything strange the night before. I was shocked when two thirds of the people raised their hands. I went around interviewing people and was amazed at the differences in their stories. Several children had seen shape-shifting ships, which changed from circular, to square, to triangular to diamond shaped and back. Others had seen glowing discs. Some had seen cylindrical shaped metallic objects. Some had received telepathic communications. A few claimed to have seen metallic discs land and others claimed to have been beamed aboard ships. Many saw lights of different shapes and sizes. Many saw Orbs. I realized that these objects are from other dimensions and what people experience depends of their own frequency, their own vibrations, their expectations and their intensions. After this mind expanding experience I have not judged anyone for what they claim to have seen, felt, or experienced.

I believe Earth has been populated, and may currently be populated, by civilizations we are not aware of. Like those who built the Nazca Lines in Peru, Stonehenge and other mysterious sacred places, advanced civilizations have come and gone. Are they still near, monitoring us? I believe they are our extraterrestrial ancestors or our future offspring. They are increasingly making their presence known. Our star brothers and sisters are supporting us as family at this time. The time has come for us to exercise our free will and magnetize an invitation to those in other dimensions willing to assist us in whatever way they can. There is a purification underway. We must accept that this purification begins within. We must purify ourselves, and our way of life. This means turning away from militarism and the industrial way of life. There are other technologies available to us that are non-polluting. The "powers that be" prevent our access to these other technologies, but they won't be able to hide them from us forever.

Since harmonic convergence, in 1987, I have seen many strange unexplained lights in the sky. I am often inspired while watching them or after having seen them. These lights inspire ideas that seem to come to me from out of the blue.

In December 2008, I began seeing a pattern appearing on walls or other flat surfaces. This pattern appeared repeatedly for over a week, in the evenings, before I'd drop off to sleep. I asked the Universe what it was. I was guided to read a book called *The Serpent of Light*. I was amazed to find a picture of the pattern I'd been seeing in this book. This pattern is called "The Flower Of Life" and is, apparently, the basic sacred geometry pattern of life from which all things are created. I've seen this pattern often ever since.

I decided to become more specific with my requests to the Universe. I sent more specific intensions out during meditation. I'd also speak my requests out loud. "OK, I know you're there but I haven't seen many of you. I'd like to see more of you soon. I invite you to be a part of my life."

I went to Fountain Creek Nature Center near my mom's house in Fountain, Colorado, to exercise. I had just finished and had lay down to rest and relax. I was flat on my back looking at the beautiful blue sky that hadn't a cloud. Suddenly a small white cloud popped into view. It did not condense and grow. One minute it wasn't there and the next moment … poof … there it was. This seemed strange to me so I decided to watch it for a while. There appeared to be a ripple of energy surrounding it similar to heat waves coming off hot pavement. As I watched, the cloud broke into two pieces – one large and one small. The larger portion of the cloud dissipated leaving the smaller portion behind. As it began to disappear I noticed a cylindrical metallic object behind it. The small cloud completely vanished leaving the dull silver/grey cylindrical object in clear view. It made no sound, did not move and had no exhaust. It was pointed on both ends and had no wings. It was visible for approximately fifteen seconds and then it just vanished. One second it was there and the next it was gone. I did not see it move or accelerate in any direction. It simply disappeared.

What I found extremely strange was that for the next three days I could see into another dimension. I don't know if this ability had anything to do with the UFO sighting, but there are no coincidences. I believe the incidents are related. What do I mean when I say "I could see into another dimension"? Let me explain.

It was during the blue moon (which is the second full moon in a calendar month) in May, 2007. I'd seen the cylindrical solid metallic object that afternoon. I was living with my mom at the time and was sitting with her in the living room watching the evening news when all of a sudden I began to see a scroll coming towards me. It looked a bit like a movie introduction, similar to the "in a galaxy far away" scroll in the movie

Star Wars. It was red, with gold sacred geometrical shapes. It was two-dimensional at first and I could see through it. I thought I might be hallucinating, though I'd never hallucinated before. I asked my mom if she could see what I was seeing. She could not. I wondered if I should go to the hospital. I called my nutritionist and according to her, as our vibrations increase and our energies shift, more and more people will begin seeing into other dimensions. This eased my mind, so I decided not to judge or discount what I was experiencing. I went with the flow without expectations.

I watched the two dimensional wave of red and gold for quite some time. It was transparent and resembled sheer cloth traveling in an arch. Then it morphed into three dimensions and took up the entire room. It was the most beautiful thing I've ever witnessed except for the Aurora Borealis (northern lights) I'd seen as a child in Alaska. I watched it for another half hour and then went back to my bedroom. I continued to watch this energy display in my room. I called in the Light Beings and my room filled with more of them. First they appeared as individual Orbs, but rapidly multiplied. They became so thick that they looked like bubbles in a bubble bath. Then they became so dense that it looked as though the room was filled with shaving cream. I realized that the Orbs I capture in my photography are around us all the time and that those that show up in pictures, do so deliberately in an effort to communicate with us. They show us we are never alone. After observing the Orbs for a long time I decided to call in my angels. As soon as I invited them, the entire room filled with angels gliding in close ranks, shoulder to shoulder. Their rows floated from the ceiling to the floor and filled the room. Just as the Orbs, they started out few in number and rapidly multiplied. There appeared to be thousands of them. They were transparent and had beautiful wings. I watched them for some time and then they faded away. The experience brought to mind the age-old question: "How many angels can fit on the head of a pin." I'd say there is no limit to their number.

Over the course of the next three days, I saw energy flowing from all living things (and sometimes even non-living things). I could not will these visions to come or go. Sometimes I could see into another dimension and other times I couldn't. At one point I went outside on my back porch and could see energy all around me. I saw energy radiating from everything, not just from plants, animals, people and clouds, but from inanimate objects like rocks and houses as well. It was breathtaking. At one point I could "see" sound coming from a jet as it passed overhead. Don't ask me how, because I don't know. I am grateful for this experiential gift from the Universe. It was a true journey into the unknown for me. I was not under the influence of any mind or mood altering substances while this occurred. The energy I saw reminded me of Kirlian photography. Perhaps I was seeing the life force contained in all things. My journey into other dimensions lasted 3 days.

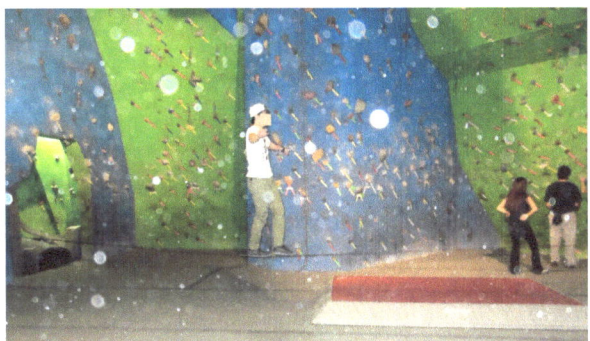
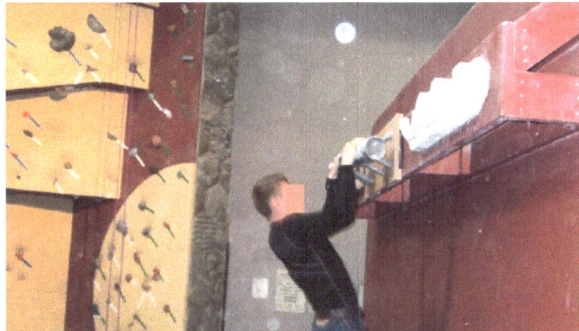
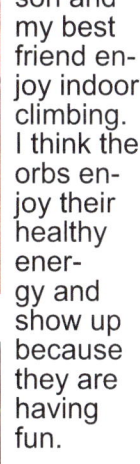

My oldest son and my best friend enjoy indoor climbing. I think the orbs enjoy their healthy energy and show up because they are having fun.

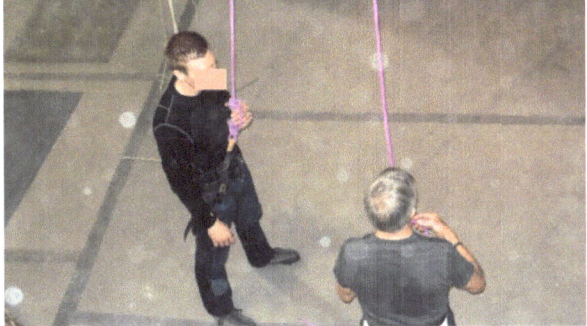
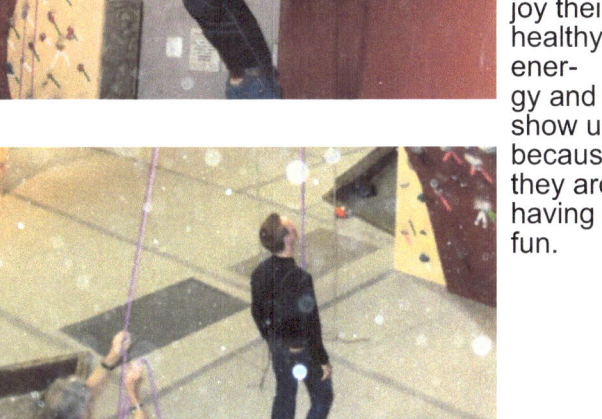

God is Light. God is Universal Mind. Mind is Light. Mind knows. Walter Russell

What is Sacred Geometry?

Mathematics is the alphabet with which God has written the universe.
– Galileo

Sacred geometry involves sacred universal patterns used in the design of everything in our reality. It is the invisible patterns that animate our physical world much as many spiritual traditions believe that the soul animates the body. This mathematical yet esoteric realm represents creation.

The belief that the universe was created according to a geometric plan has ancient origins. Legends of ancient high cultures such as the Egyptian Temple Science indicate how advanced - and how secret - this geometric information was in earlier times. Perhaps the ancients had good reason to keep this information secret. The information can be dangerous. For example: the same geometric form known and kept very secret by the Greeks over 2500 years ago (because they said it could cause great destruction if misused) is shown in modern declassified military documents to be the exact same shape used to create the world's first atomic bomb.

"In nature, we find patterns, designs and structures from the most minuscule particles, to expressions of life discernible by human eyes, to the greater cosmos. These inevitably follow geometrical models and examples, which reveal to us the nature of each form and its vibrational resonances. They are also symbolic of the underlying metaphysical principle of the inseparable relationship of the part to the whole. It is this principle of oneness underlying all geometry that permeates the architecture of all form in its myriad diversity. This principle of interconnectedness, inseparability and union provides us with a continuous reminder of our relationship to the whole, a blueprint for the mind to the sacred foundation of all things created." (Rawles, 2008)

The majority of Light Beings I've photographed appear to be three-dimensional spheres. The sphere may be the simplest and most perfect of forms. The sphere is an ultimate expression of unity, completeness, and integrity. There is no point of view given greater or lesser importance, and all points on the surface are equally accessible and regarded by the center from which all originate. Atoms, cells, seeds, planets, and globular star systems all echo the spherical paradigm of total inclusion, acceptance, simultaneous potential and fruition, the macrocosm and microcosm.

After the sphere, the next common Light Being that shows up appears to be a circle. These circles may simply be spheres from a different perspective. The circle is a two-dimensional shadow of the sphere which is regarded throughout cultural history as an icon of the ineffable oneness; the indivisible fulfillment of the Universe. All other symbols and geometries reflect various aspects of the profound and consummate per-fection of the circle, sphere and other higher dimensional forms of these we might imagine. In the language of sacred symbolism, the essence of the circle exists in a dimension that transcends the linear rationality that it contains.

The principle of sacred geometry includes the circle as its principal element since it lies at the heart of the creative principle. It's the representation of cosmic life, from the smallest atom to the largest planet. All things are divided from within itself so, paradoxically, all things are contained within it. It is therefore the symbol of the unknowable, of Spirit and of heaven.

Many of the round Light Beings that appear in my photography have a center, as in the "bulls eye" type. At the center of a circle or a sphere is always an infinitesimal point. The point needs no dimension, yet embraces all dimension. Transcendence of the illusions of time and space result in the point of here and now, which is our most primal light of consciousness. The proverbial "light at the end of the tunnel" is being validated by the ever-increasing literature on so-called "near-death experiences". If our essence is truly spiritual omnipresence, then perhaps the point of our being here is to recognize the oneness we share, by by seeing all individuals as equally precious and sacred aspects of the One.

Indelibly etched on the walls of the Osirion temple at Abydos, Egypt, the Flower of Life contains a vast Akashic system of information, including templates for the five Platonic Solids. I had no idea the signifi-cance of the Flower of Life when I first saw it appear to me, as mentioned previously.

Sacred Geometry by Leonardo Da Vinci

Many of the ancients deeply studied sacred geometry and it's connection to the creation of physical reality as well as consciousness. One of the most well known is Italy's master artist and inventor, Leonardo Da Vinci. These drawings are all by Leonardo. It is obvious that he was fascinated by Sacred Geometry, and more specifically, The Flower of Life.

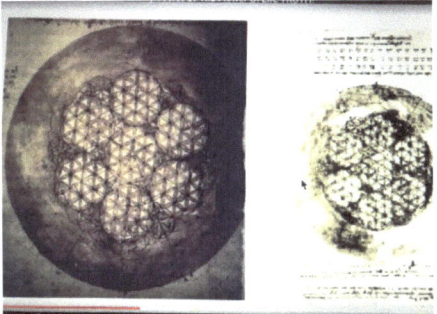 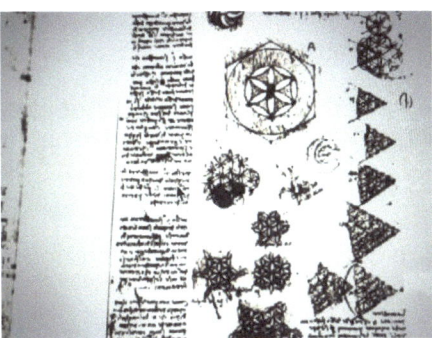 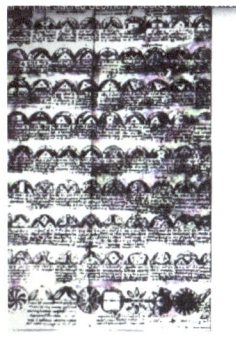 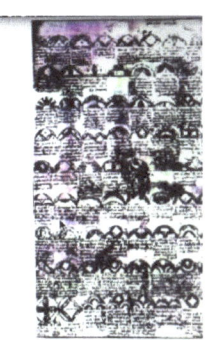

Sacred Geometry is important and relevant to us today because it reflects the fractal and holographic nature of consciousness. Fractals, found in nature, are self-similar patterns that repeat in both the small and large scale. The phrase "as above, so below" is an expression of a fractal reality that points to the truth of our divine nature being reflected in a physical reality, even if we have not yet learned to recognize or embrace it.

Consciousness is holographic. Put simply, a hologram reflects fractal principles because its properties repeat, no matter how large or small the image. For instance, a hologram of a tree may physically be cut into several pieces. But upon closer examination of the hologram, the complete image of the tree will still be present in every piece, no matter how small -- theoretically, even beyond the physical and into the quantum level.

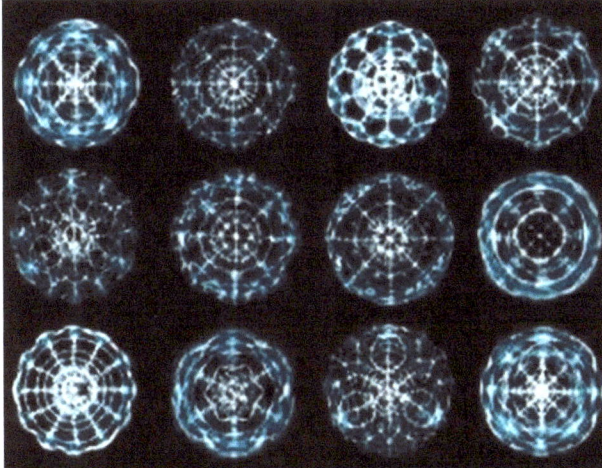

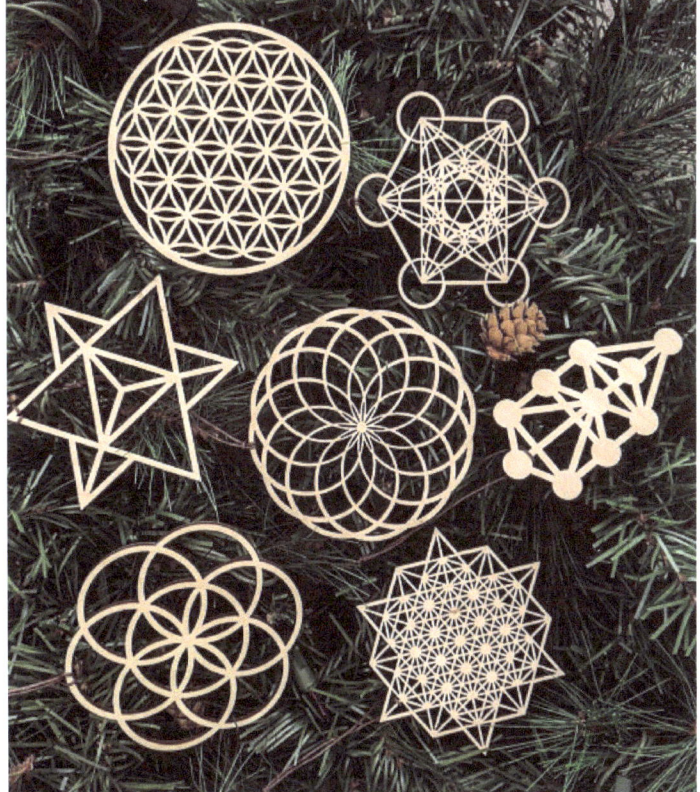

Cymatics is a study in the field of physics of wave phenomena, especially sound waves, and their visual representations. The illustration above shows Cymatic Waves generated by sound. Cymatics can also be used as a therapy in which sound waves are directed at the body with the aim of promoting health. It is interesting to note that sound waves create scared geometrical patterns. The picture to the right shows sacred geometrical shapes.

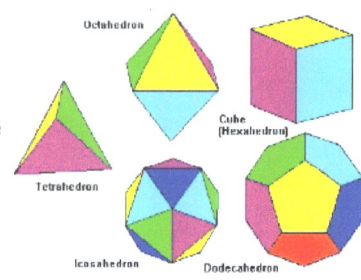

The Platonic Solids are the names given to the five "perfect shapes" formed when dividing a sphere into three-dimensional forms, with each division having the exact same shape and angle. The polygons are named after the Greek philosopher Plato. There are five (and only five) Platonic solids. These are: 1) the tetrahedron which has four faces, each of which is an equilateral triangle; 2) the hexahedron, or cube, which consists of six square faces; 3) the octahedron which has eight faces of equilateral triangles; 4) the dodecahedron which has twelve faces of pentagons; and 5) The icosahedron which has twenty faces, each of which is an equilateral triangle.

The Greeks taught that these five solids were the core patterns of physical creation. Four of the solids were seen as the archetypal patterns behind the four elements (earth, air, fire, and water), while the fifth was held to be the pattern behind the life force itself, the Greeks' ether. These same shapes are intimately related to the arrangements of protons and neutrons in the elements of the periodic table.

Robert J. Gilbert, Ph.D., became aware of Sacred Geometry through an unusual route: he was an Instructor in the U.S. Marine Corps, in the field of Nuclear, Biological, and Chemical Warfare Survival in the early 1980's. He learned that behind all the systems of modern technology and all the forces of Nature were specific patterns, which were being avidly studied by both scientists and by governments. Alongside the usual mathematical studies of modern science, there exists a thriving sub-culture of advanced scientists studying pure structural patterns as a key to everything from Nuclear Physics to Human Biology. Dr. Gilbert was surprised to find studies commissioned by Governments, and even by NATO, which analyzed the pure pattern information of natural systems. It became apparent to him that much of modern cutting-edge technology was coming out of these pattern studies. The new field of Nano-technology - in which human beings are now able to create any kind of matter, by creating structures at the molecular level, opens doors for amazing new discoveries.

The foundation of all life and all creation is this geometric language in nature, which modern science is currently using to tap the powers of nature in modern technology. All modern technology is based on the twin variables of shape and material; different shapes create different energetic effects, just as different materials offer a full spectrum of different useful energy qualities. Shape is really a pattern of energy movement frozen in space, a pattern which nature gives a specific power.

Crop circles are excellent examples of sacred geometry. Orbs are often seen in the vicinity of crop circles before, during and after their creation. There are YouTube videos showing Orbs creating crop circles within seconds. Here is a link to one in a YouTube video entitled MINDBLOWING: Crop Circle Filmed Being Formed In SECONDS By Mystery Balls Of Light: https://www.express.co.uk/news/weird/842579/UFO-crop-circle-made-ball-of-light-aliens I believe this footage is authentic. It shows two bright Orbs flying over a field while just below them, within seconds, a crop circle is carved into the crop. I've seen still shots of Orbs around the circles, but never one with them in motion like this, showing the miracle occurring. Crop circles have been marginalized by practically the entire scientific community since they challenge the current world view simply because science is at odds to explain them.

It is interesting that today we find ourselves at the final crossroads in our evolution. Since that day when we decided to abandon our faith in the universal way and follow the mechanical codes of science our consciousness has shifted from one of reverence for all things sacred to the worship of abstract materialism. Consequently, our change of attitude has endangered our living, breathing celestial sphere. Perhaps that's why crop circles, with their foundations based squarely upon sacred geometry, have chosen to appear at this particular point in time. They remind us that if we observe the fundamental laws of the universe we may still be in time to discover the secrets of universal harmony and salvage our very own symbol of eternal life, the Earth. Perhaps the crop circles infuse the energy of their patterns into the Earth to help raise the vibration of the planet, or to help it heal from the abuse humans have perpetrated.

Crop Circles are Sacred Geometical Shapes

Who or what is creating them?

Do their shapes influence our planet?

Are they encoded messages for mankind?

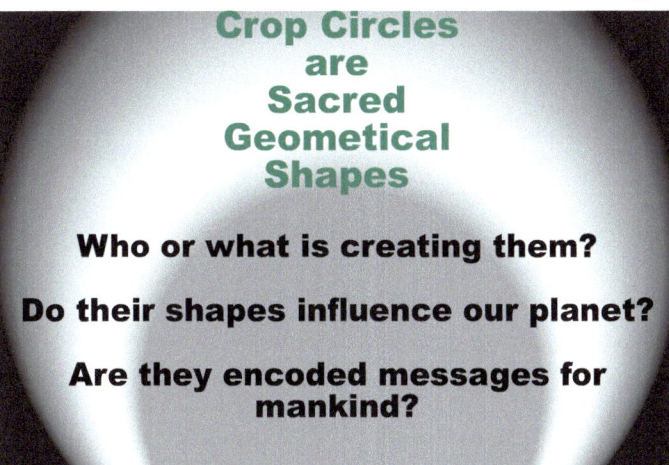

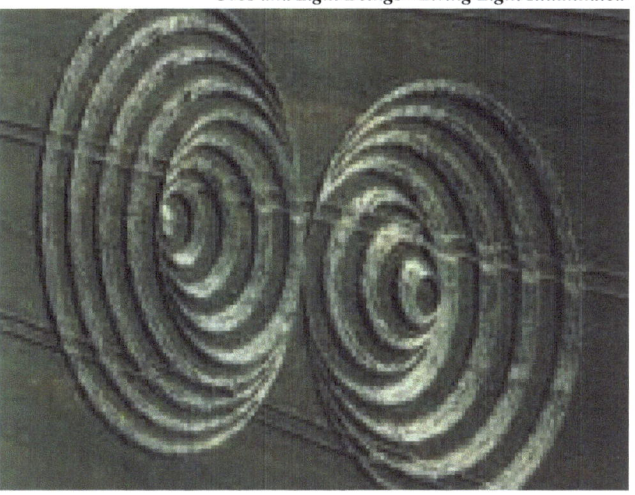

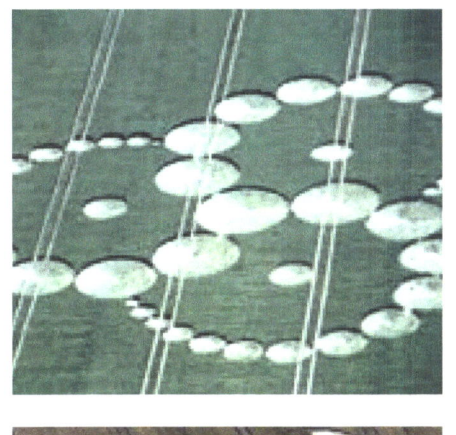

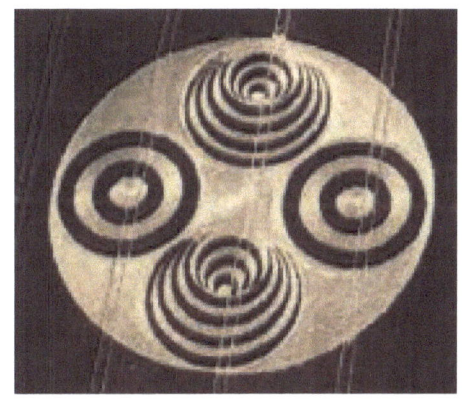

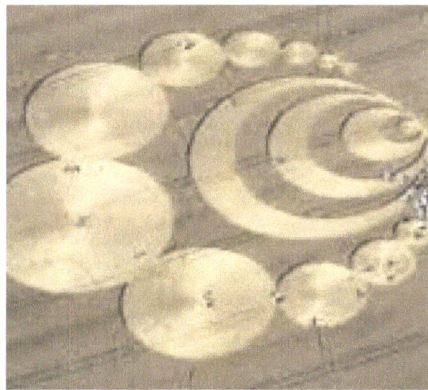

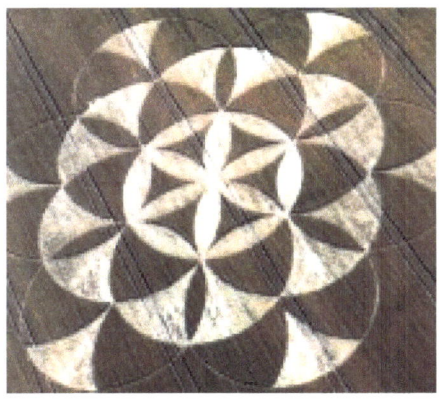

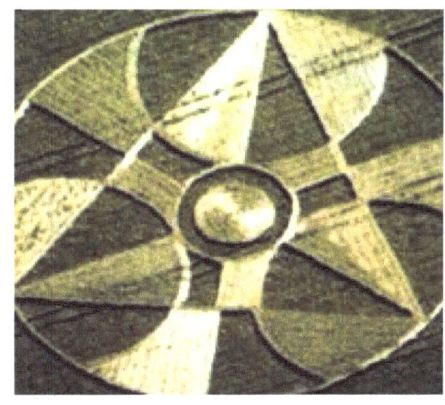

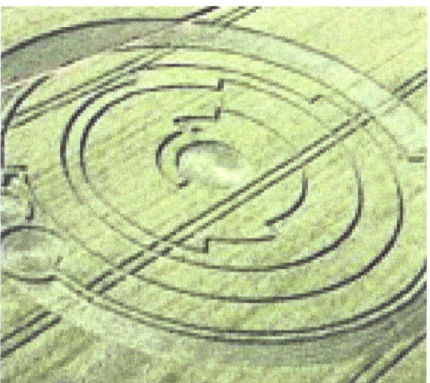

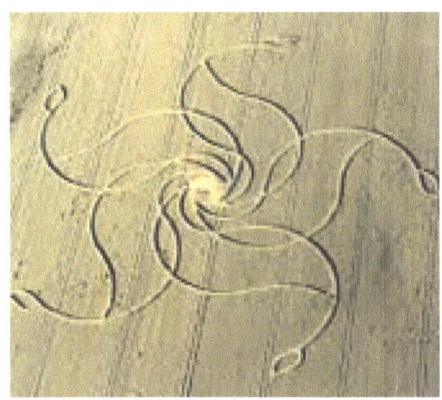

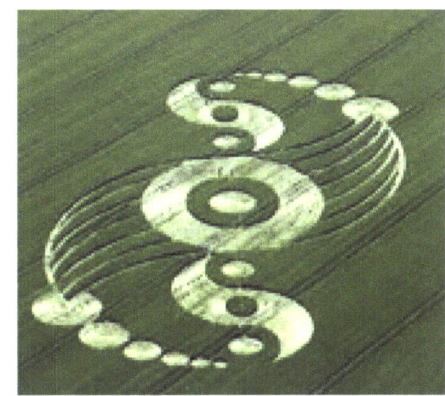

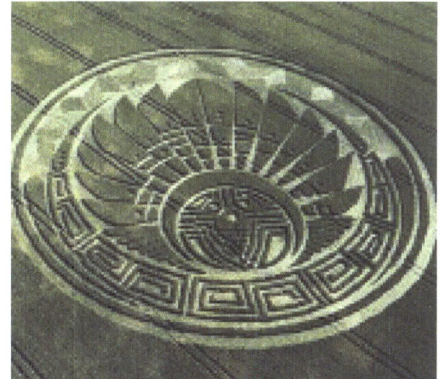

Ephesians 5:14 All things that are exposed are made manifest by the Light: for whatsoever doth make manifest is Light.

The Coral Castle

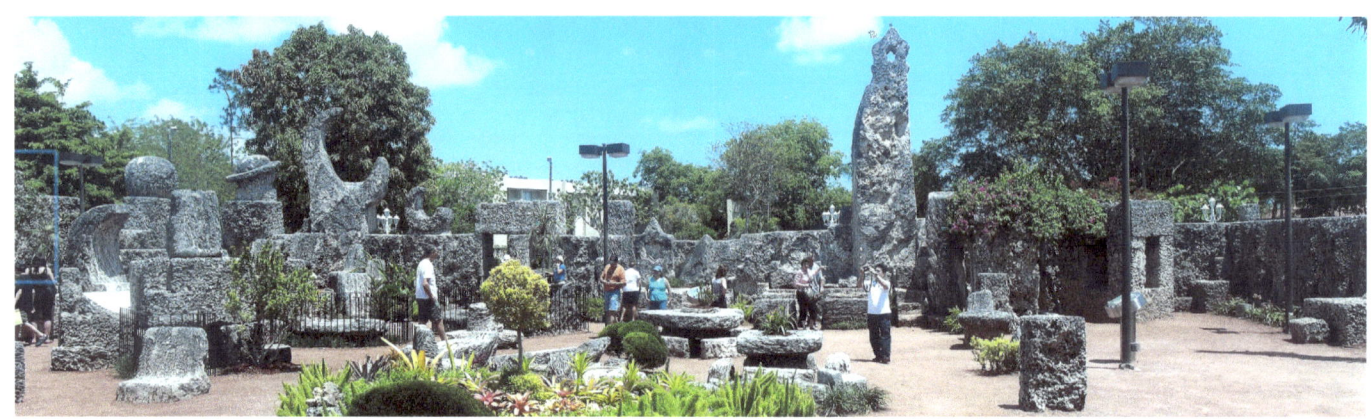

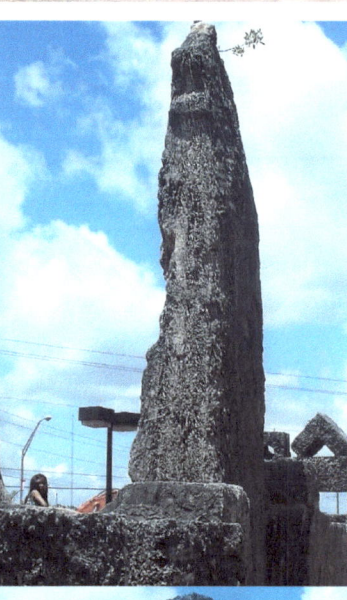

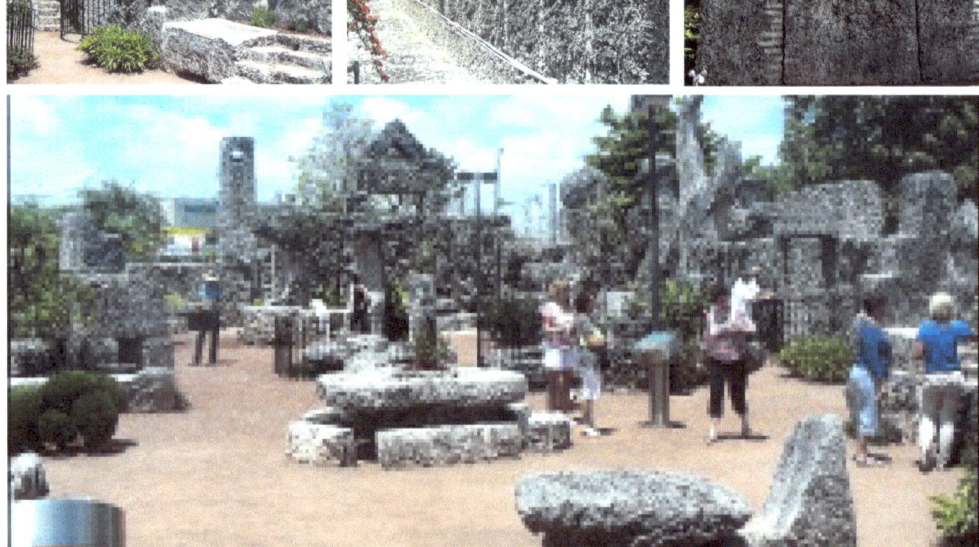

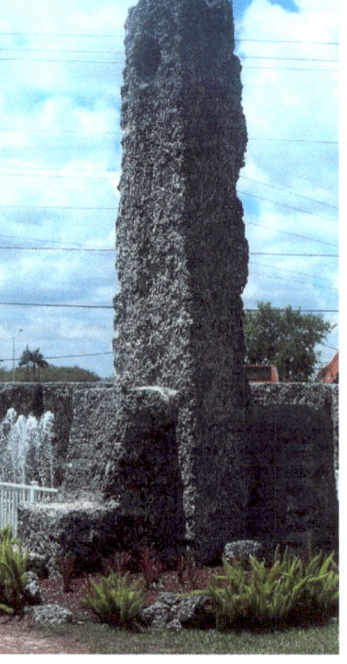

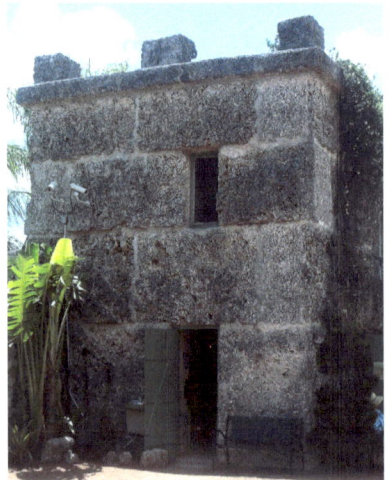

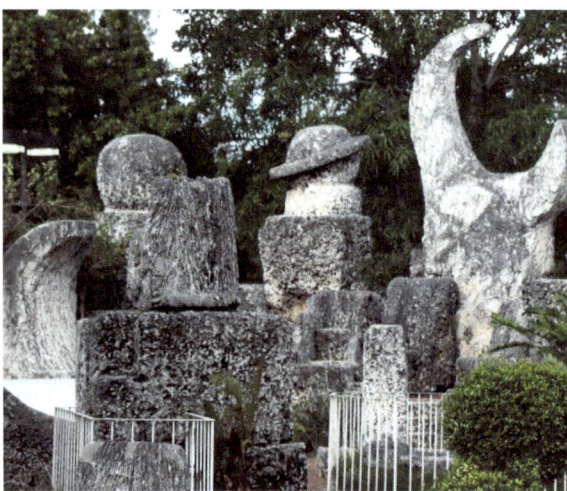

Edward Leedskalnin (1887-1951) was a Latvian emigrant to the United States, self-taught engineer and sculptor who single-handedly built the Coral Castle in Florida. Not really coral, the huge stones that comprise the castle are composed of limestone; the coral designation came about later when visitors noticed fossilized coral and shells in some of the rocks. The average weight of the stones is about 14 tons each. Using no joint compound or mortar, the massive stones, when combined together, are held in place by their own weight. With these huge rocks, Leedskalnin built walls, erected a tower and a 22-ton obelisk. He made a variety of furniture including beds and rocking chairs, as well as a fountain, table, well, sundial and throne. They are so well constructed (and heavy), that during Category 5 Hurricane Andrew in 1992, none of the stones shifted and the eight foot high wall around the castle remains of uniform height to this day. No one ever saw how he was able to cut and move huge blocks weighing tons. He single handedly moved the entire castle to a new location after he built it. When asked how he manipulated such large blocks alone, Leedskalnin would explain that he had "discovered the secrets of the pyramids." He is said to have used reverse magnetism. He died without disclosing his secrets, but he may have had help from some very intelligent beings. Perhaps he was taught to use his consciousness to create miracles. Parts of the Castle look identical to megalithic structures I've visited in Mexico and Peru. I believe they were similarly constructed. Perhaps Leedskalnin provides a link to ancient knowledge that will soon be revealed. I look forward to learning more.

Leedskalnin saw things very similar to what Grace Butler sees. I include a quote by him here:

"Biologists might be interested to know that I believe I can see chromosomes without a microscope. At least, I think what I am seeing may be chromosomes. To see them I close my eyes and then I open one just a little and look at the blue sky. I can then see chains of beads floating in the liquid of my eye. Some chains of beads are longer than others. Most of the chains are folded over in irregular shapes. Between several beads in a chain there is a bigger bead. Sometimes there are beads hanging outside the chain, and sometimes I can see beads floating separately. Each bead's center is light, and the outside rim is dark. If I open my eye a little more and look sharper, then I can see round shining things running in every direction in jumpy paths. Some leave shiny waves, like a path, before they disappear. Each shiny thing is many times smaller than the smallest bead. They are not crowded, they all travel at the same speed, but that speed is too fast for clear observation. To see finer things, I look into a gray cloud with my eye open until I see a darker spot. When the spot begins to boil in the middle, I can see tiny multi-colored streaks running out of the middle. The scene lasts about a minute. When it is over I never know when I'll see it again.

I believe that every form of existence, whether it is a rock, tree or animal, has a beginning and an end. The three things that all matter is constructed of have no beginning and no end. I believe they are the North and South Pole individual magnets, and the neutral particles of matter. These three things are the construction blocks of everything. Consciousness holds everything together."

I believe the Coral Castle was built using cosmic concrete and consciousness. Consciousness manifested, formed and shaped the stones. Were the stones and coral teleported and mixed on site? Leedskalnin may have had help from something or someone else. If he did have help, it wasn't from a human, I'll guarantee you. What intrigues me, is that I've seen construction just like the Coral Castle in Peru and Mexico. Examples of similar construction are presented below.

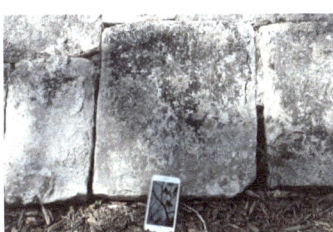
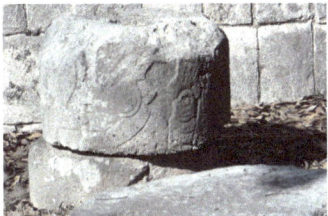
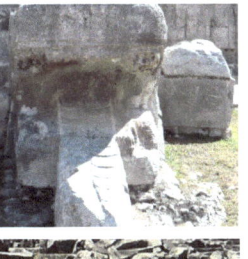
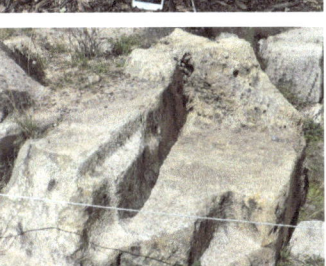
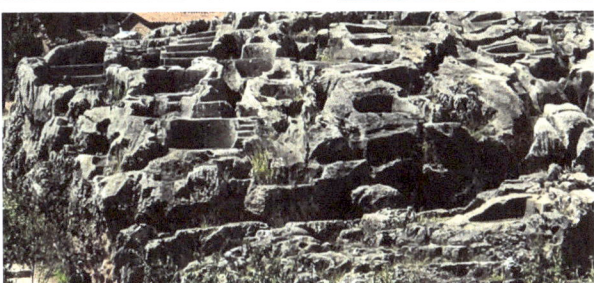

The top three pictures are from Chichen Itza, Mexico, and the bottom two are from the Cusco area of Peru. I believe consciousness and cosmic concrete were used to manifest these amazing structures. It looks like the Coral Castle and these examples may have employed the same method of construction. Did someone or something teach the ancient construction method to Leedskalnin? Was he assisted by the unseen? Was a similar construction method used in Egypt? Maybe the "matter manipulation methods" used by our global ancient ancestors was once again used at Coral Castle. Perhaps those methods will soon be revealed, since they've been recently demonstrated.

"Friendship is the purest love. It is the highest form of Love where nothing is asked for, no condition, where one simply enjoys giving." Osho

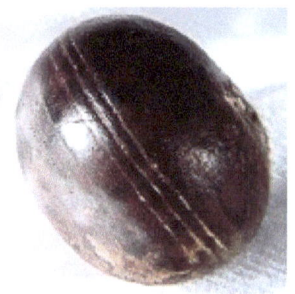

Klerksdorp Sphere from S. Africa, 2.8 billion years old.

Deep in the mines of South Africa approximately 200 metallic spheres (Klerksdorp spheres) from 2.2 to 10 cm in diameter were found in a silver mine in the eastern Transvaal Ottosoal, South Africa. These round spherical balls are made of unexplained solid blue metal, but do contain hematite. There has been fervent attempted debunking by the scientific community concerning these objects. Geologists have attempted to debunk these artifacts as natural formations or "limonite concretions". They fail to explain sufficiently how these formations occurred naturally with perfectly straight and perfectly spaced grooves around the centers. Could these be representations of orbs? The Orb shot at the right looks very similar to the South African photo on the left.

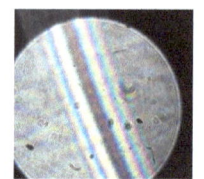

"Roelf Marx, curator of the museum of Klerksdorp, South Africa, where some of the spheres are housed, said: 'the spheres are a complete mystery. They look man-made, yet at the time in Earth's history when they came to rest in this rock no intelligent life existed (according to whom?). The globes are very hard and cannot be scratched, even by steel." (Andrews, 1993)

"Evolutionists refuse to accept them as to do so would mean re-evaluating their whole indoctrinated belief system. They will even stoop to produce outright fantasy in their attempts to discredit these discoveries. If that fails then they will just pretend that they do not exist, and then hide them away – forever." Monte Aldone

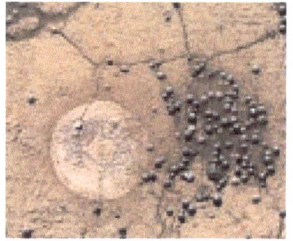

Blueberry spheres on Mars.

3/25/04 This image from the Mars Exploration Rover Opportunity's panoramic camera is an approximate true-color rendering of the exceptional rocks called the Berry Bowl in the Eagle Crater outcropping. The study of this "blueberry-strewn" area and the identification of hematite as the major iron-bearing element within these sphere-like grains helped scientists confirm their hypothesis that the hematite in these Martian spherules was deposited in water.

The NASA Curiosity rover has spotted a unique round rock on the red planet. Nasa said it was probably an example of Martian concretion, the process of compacting and hardening a mass of matter.

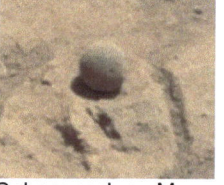

Sphere rock on Mars

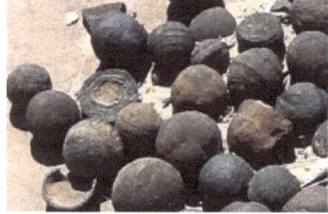

Moqui Marbles are found in Utah and Aizona, USA.

Moqui Marbles are found in Utah, USA. Moqui Marble is the term used to identify a marble-like concretion having a sandstone center encased in an iron oxide shell. These geological oddities litter the surface of the iron rich Navajo sandstone in southern Utah's Zion and Capitol national parks, Grand Staircase-Escalante National Monument, Snow Canyon State Park and the Moab area. They are also found in Arizona. They resemble the blueberry rocks on mars. Is there a connection?

Moqui Marbles

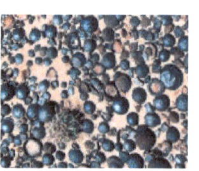

These two photos below are of a rock I bought at a flea market. I believe it is a Moqui Marble. It's odd perfect shape with a perfectly symmetrical circular interior is interesting. What do the cuts in it mean? Was this worn as a piece of jewelry? Who cut the grooves? How long ago?

Pictures of my specimen which I believe to be a Moqui Marble.

Large spheres are found globally and defy explaination.

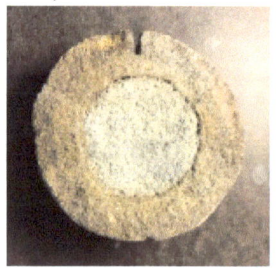
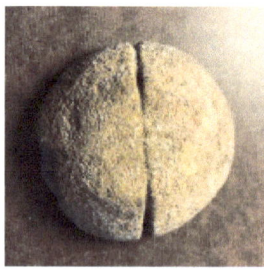
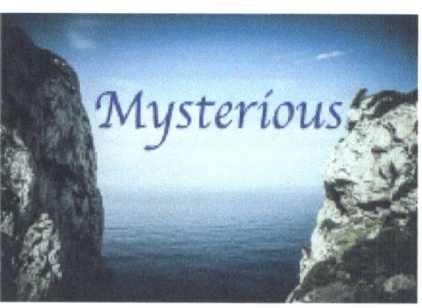
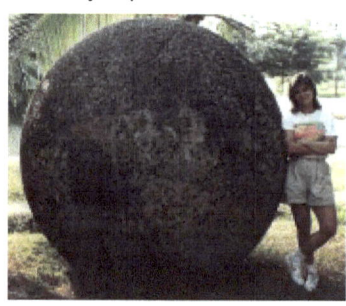

What is Kirlian Photography?

These images were made using Kirlian photography. This is a technique for recording photographic images of corona discharges and the auras of living creatures. The camera and the subject interact to produce a corona of multi-frequency energy waves - from low infrared to well past the visible spectrum.

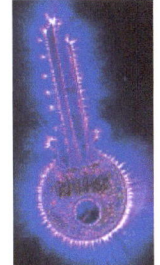

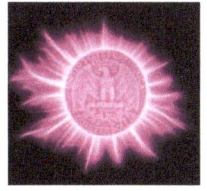

Kirlian photography can also produce images of corona discharges emitted from inanimate objects. A corona discharge is an electrical discharge brought on by the ionization of a fluid such as air surrounding a conductor that is electrically charged. The fact that glowing auras are seen around non-living objects as well as living objects in Kirlian photos, is often simply ignored. Is this electrical charge a manifestation of subtle energy? If so, why disregard the fact that inanimate objects radiate some form of subtle energy?

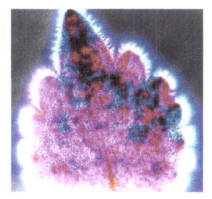

In Kirlian photography, high voltage, high frequency electricity produces a discharge through the air between an electro plate and an object. Light energy (photons) coming from this discharge can be recorded on photographic film placed between the object and the electrified plate. Effectively this produces a record of ´photon´ emissions referred to as an 'Aura'.

Semyon Davidovich Kirlian believed that images created by Kirlian photography depict a theoretical energy field, or aura, thought, by some, to surround all living things. Kirlian and his wife were convinced that their images showed a life force or energy field that reflected the physical and emotional states of their living subjects. They thought that these images could be used to diagnose illnesses.

Scientists have explored the idea of a human biofield using Kirlian photography research, attempting to explain a vitalistic energy or subtle energy (Chi) that permeates all living things. Vitalism refers to the theory that the origin and phenomena of life are dependent on a force or principle distinct from purely chemical or physical forces. The idea of Chi as its own field, not simply a creature's electromagnetic field, has been mostly disregarded by the scientific community. All living creatures generate and emit radiations. Photons of light, electromagnetic frequencies, heat, sound, and scent are all emitted from our bodies in direct relationship to our internal states. This remarkable, subtle system of exchange contains a wealth of information. Why do most scientists dismiss this mysterious energy?

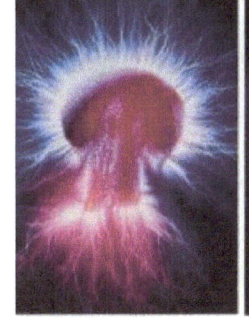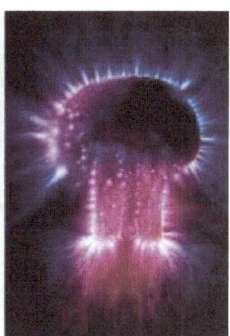

Organic   Commercial

Kirlian photographs reveal unique insights into unseen energy fields. The difference between a Kirlian photo of raw organic food verses one of cooked food is dramatic. Organically grown food has more life force energy than commercially grown food. That's a fact, proven by Kirlian photography.

Cooked Tomato   Raw Tomato   Cooked Broccoli Raw Broccoli

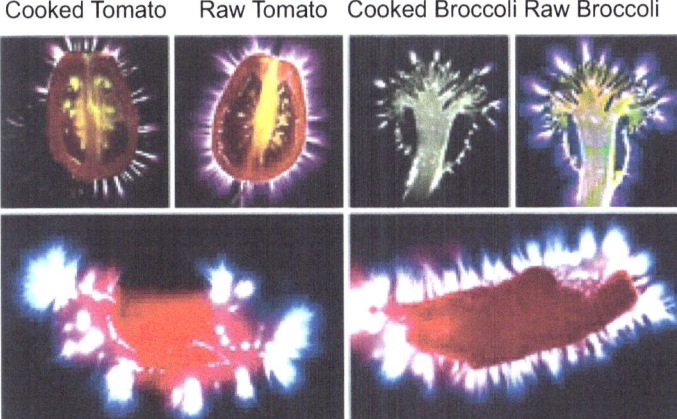

Cooked Meat (medium rare)   Raw Meat

Raw food has more life force energy than cooked food. The cooking process reduces the life force energy of food. I expect Kirlian photos of genetically modified foods compared to natural foods would be dramatic as well.

Gary Pooke and Paul Sparks were researchers at the U.S. Naval postgraduate school in the Man/Machine Systems Design Lab in Monterey, California. They researched Kirlian photography and their conclusion was that the technique has possible uses in the diagnosis of psychopathology, psychology, medicine and agriculture. It can detect diseases such as gout and rheumatoid arthritis. The application of Kirlian techniques may become a valuable diagnostic dimension in some clinical applications, in the near future. To a large extent, it has been used in alternative medicine research.

Leading scientists in the field of quantum physics are now aware that this mysterious energy field contains secrets about the way our bodies and minds operate. We begin to consider that our bodies are shimmering light. We are, in fact, seeing more of ourselves.

"We need instruments which extend our physical senses and help us to 'see' what is going on at some deeper level. Microbiology achieves this. So does Magnetic Resonance Imaging (MRI) scanning. MRIs only stimulate the atoms of the physical body through 'resonance'. Kirlian imagery goes one step beyond by stimulating the atoms of the more subtle 'etheric' body. Although this field is on a higher frequency spectrum than physical matter, it is able to affect the behavior of subatomic particles of physical matter such as electrons." (Broom, 2018)

A similar application of Kirlian technique is Gas Discharge Visualization (GDV). GDV does not involve a photographic process. It employs state of the art fiberglass optics, a digitalized TV Matrix and image processing with sophisticated computer software. The image is transferred to a computer in a digital form. This means that the image can be reviewed scientifically. Certain parameters can be quantified. It can be used to pinpoint any interruption of the energy field surrounding an organ or connected with the circuitry of that organ. It quantifies the changes which are observed in a scientific way. One cannot underestimate the importance of being able to measure the electromagnetic disturbances in the meridian system.

The meridian system extends throughout the entire body and carries Chi (life-force/subtle energy); the meridian concept is central to acupuncture and other forms of oriental medicine, and has been used for healing for over 5,000 years. Mainstream Western medicine has been frustrated by its inability to verify the presence of meridians. They are also challenged by the verification of the presence of Chi.

Extensive use of the GDV teaches us that nothing happens in isolation and when disease invades the body. all systems of the body are affected. It is possible to discover where diseases originate in the body and also to track and monitor the whole process of pathology from its development to its removal using GDV. Our cells are guided by energetic patterns of a higher frequency. We may not be able to quantify or measure that higher frequency at this time, but we can monitor its influence.

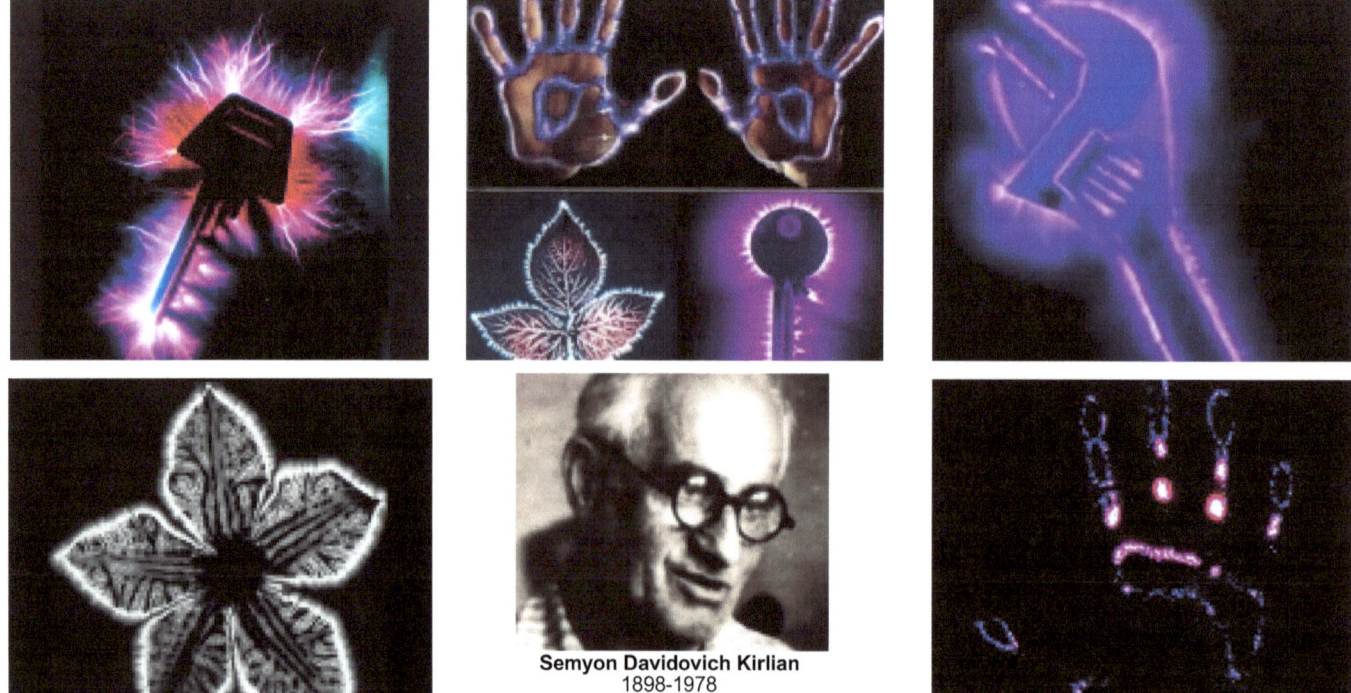

Semyon Davidovich Kirlian
1898-1978
Russian Electrician who invented
Kirlian Photography

Ecclesiastes 2:13 Light exceeds (outshines) darkness.

How I Began Seeing Light as Orbs
By Grace Butler

Authors' note: Grace Butler calls all the different varieties of Light she photographs "Orbs". Some are what I call Orbs, shaped as spheres Authors' note: Grace Butler calls all the different varieties of Light she photographs "Orbs". Some are what I call Orbs, shaped as spheres or circles. Others are what I refer to as "Light Beings". Orbs are Light Beings, but not all Light Beings are Orbs. Grace has captured unique shapes and expressions of Light that defy definition. I've taken the liberty of substituting "Living Light" or "Light Being" for "Orbs" when I felt it appropriate while editing.

Something unusual first caught my eye in 2008. I saw it on the surface of the water. As I looked at it I began to realize that it was not something in the water. It led me on the search that I am still on today.

I have had many paranormal experiences in my life since the mid 90's. I first started communicating with Spirit by means of automatic writing. I was inspired to read many books by mystics and learned much. I've read many of these books for my subscribers to listen to on my YouTube channel. I wanted others to hear and understand what I was learning. I came to understand that my intentions must be pure. Pure intentions are those with no expectation of gaining power or glory from what I learn and share.

My introduction to Light began one day when I was sitting in the sun by the pool. I could see a little "tube like thing" that seemed to be on the surface of the water. I began to see these things in the air. I would see them when I was in the sun or in a brightly lit room. When I spoke of this to my family they did not understand. It was logical that they were not interested because what I was experiencing was foreign to them.

I continued to look at the empty space between my eyes and what I was seeing in the background. The Orbs became clearer as I continued to practice this for several months. If I tightly squinted my right eye and looked at the space lit up by sunlight or in a brightly lit room, I found that by allowing only a small amount of Light to enter my eye, I could see them better. They reminded me of a raindrop running down a window. They were transparent, yet had outlines. They did not move like raindrops falling in one direction. These tubes moved in many different directions. I saw more of them as I continued to look at them over a period of time. They moved in a zigzag manner, but they always stayed in front of my eyes. Is this what Leedskalin describes on page 39?

My daughter-in-law wanted me to see an eye doctor. She thought I might have 'floaters'. Floaters are microscopic fibers in the eye that cast tiny shadows on the retina. The shadows one sees are called floaters. I knew I was not seeing floaters because I only saw them when I would squint my eyes hoping to see them. If I was not squinting, I did not see them.

I began sitting on the porch in the evening when the sun was low in the sky and I would look at the sunlight. I started to see different things of various configurations. Sometimes I'd see tubular things and other times I'd see things which intertwined.

I've been guided by spirit to take pictures of Light. The methods I use have been inspired. Using my Kodak Easy Share Z710 AF 10 X Optical Zoom digital camera, I attempted to capture what I was witnessing. An external creative impulse led me to focus on Light reflecting from shiny spots. I used my camera without its flash. I'd zoom in on a shiny spot of Light gleaming off a highly reflective surface. I could see an Orb through my camera's view screen when I zoomed in on the shiny Light spot. I discovered that LED Light worked best. Focusing my zoomed camera on these shiny spots of Light brought more and more Orbs into view over time.

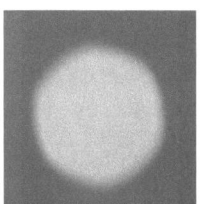 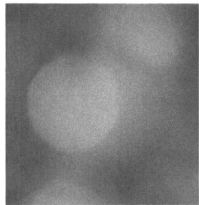 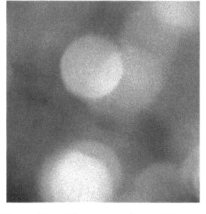

The author took these shots attempting to duplicate methods used by Grace Butler. My first shots, mostly black and white, shown here, were taken with my cell phone. Grace uses her digital camera exclusively to take all her photographs.

I first saw weird tubes with my naked eye. One day I was led to stare into the LED Light without a camera, with my eyes squinted almost shut. This allowed only a small amount of Light to enter my eye. I saw a large Orb, which moved about, opening and closing itself. This made it difficult for me to examine it because it was a moving target. I trained my eye to stay squinted open.

The Orb I saw was half a circle. It had spiky edges and had tubes and "worm like things" moving around inside of it. The Orb looked like water. I could see strange lines, tubes and circles inside of it. Some of the Orbs

I saw over time had concentric circles, black holes and white holes, all of which moved inside the Orb. The Orbs were black, white and shades of grey.

Another day I was looking at an Orb and saw two flaps on the side of it. It looked like a small 'flap' was biting into the larger Orb. I noticed that the movement of this flap corresponded to the movement of my physical eye. When I would close my eye slightly, it closed slightly. When I opened my eye wider, it opened wider. I thought, "This must be what is called the third eye". When I used my right eye this flap appeared to be biting the big Orb on the right side. When I used my left eye the flap appeared to be biting the big Orb on the left side.

I found that the best reflective surface to use for observing Orbs was glass. I began to see planes of exceptionally beautiful colors of Light. Their patterns reminded me of a peacocks' tail. I noticed little colorful bubbles forming on the edges of the flap. They multiplied and then went into the big Orb. Gradually more things merged with the large Orb. The colorful bubbles would swirl together in one direction and then stop and swirl in the opposite direction. Everything within the big Orb was showing color now. I thought, maybe it is we ourselves who color the world around us.

I began to see very long tubes filled with lines. They reminded me of fiber optics inside a wire. None of the shapes interfered with each other as they moved inside the Orb. It appeared that different shapes were on separate levels. The colors increased and what looked like molten lava moved in beautiful waves of color. It became easier to see this large Orb anytime I looked at the LED Light. I felt no one else would understand unless they saw it for themselves. I told others about it but they were not interested and maybe thought I was a bit crazy. I took more and more pictures of the Light. The colors became increasingly more vivid. The Light appeared to respond to my love of color by increasing their numbers and becoming more colorful and with vivid brilliance. They responded to my love visually. I believe they communicated with me in this way because of my love for seeing them.

I now have thousands of pictures of these Orbs, this Living Light. I continue to see the large Orb open up for me when I look into the Light. I found myself falling in love with this Light.

One day when I was looking into the Light, I traveled, in an out of body state, into the Orb. It was like I was visually swimming through seaweed. I journeyed past long strands of tubes that resembled seaweed, until I focused on one tube in particular. An opening appeared on both sides of the long tube and a section of the tubes' interior was removed for me to see. I was shown what was running through the interior of the tubes. It looked like tiny Nano crystals or diamonds were in motion. I now share what I see on my YouTube channel (Grace Butler). I've been sharing for many years. I know I am helping people because of the positive and supportive comments I receive from my viewers in response to my pictures and videos. I've posted videos showing them in motion. They appear to stretch and crawl when moving. I now have thousands of photos and videos of these breathtaking Orbs and their movement. They are alive.

Living Light changes shape as though it were a contortionist. It can spread out and look identical to a fan. It can stretch like a rubber band. Some Light Beings resemble lace or fabric. It was apparent to me that I was looking into other dimensions. Have these other dimensions of Light been explored by modern man?

I've learned much by reading books on topics that are not taught in school. I watch informative videos on subjects that fascinate me, created by people I respect. The mainstream media report little about these phenomena. I hope this book opens their eyes, and that they begin to increase their coverage of Orbs and Living Light. When scientists see these pictures, I hope they become excited about the possibilities they represent. Living Light must be studied. Claude Swanson, Ph.D., is a quantum physicist who is not afraid to venture into the subject of Light and 'consciousness'. I am encouraged by his research and look forward to more of his colleagues becoming involved. It's time to scientifically explore these other dimensions that include Living Light. My hope is that serious scientific research continues to expand on this subject.

I repeatedly saw specific patterns emerge. These patterns multiplied themselves within the Orbs. I had never filmed anything symmetrical within the Orbs before, but this new pattern was different. Symmetry was beginning to form within the Orb. I believe I was witnessing evolution within the Orbs. Perhaps I was observing a form of creation.

My previous Orb pictures had little symmetry. Nevertheless, they were very beautiful. This repeating pattern was different. It was evolving. I don't know how else to describe what was happening as I watched. Order was being created out of remarkably beautiful chaos. Something was happening, and I was able to witness its formational stages. I called this new pattern I was seeing, "curved lined balls". They morphed into many different colors. They multiplied themselves and filled the entire Orb.

John Hagelin, Ph.D., is a renowned quantum physicist. Dr. Hagelin has conducted pioneering research at the European Center for Particle Physics and at the Stanford Linear Accelerator Center. He is responsible for the development of a highly successful grand Unified Field Theory based on the superstring. In addition, Dr. Hagelin has spent much of the past twenty-five years leading a scientific investigation into the foundations of human consciousness. Dr. Hagelin, when speaking of the quantum world, said that "the universe percolates rubber bands." Rubber bands are circular. He realizes the significance of circles in the universe. There are many circles in the Orbs. What is the connection?

I think the vast outer reaches and great expanses of the universe resemble what is microscopic. Stated another way: as above, so below, and as below, so above. What is seen in something small can also be seen in something very large.

I never expected my attention would be totally captured by my discoveries. I know Light is intelligent because it communicates through pictures. It can and does communicate with me.

I believe that Living Light is here to help mankind. I think it (they?) are here to teach us to help ourselves. We must change our thinking. Have Orbs and Light Beings always been with us? Will they always be here? I believe they have been and always will be.

We (Elizabeth and I) are not trying to convince anyone of anything. This evidence is presented so that people can consider it and draw their own conclusions. People need to pay attention to messengers who are attempting to wake people up. Humanity has help from the unseen world. This unseen world is now clearly making itself known. It is no longer unseen. We are never alone. Living Light surrounds us and is inside us.

Those who use their knowledge and power to keep this information from the public won't succeed for long. Light is information. Do your part to share this information. Become interested. Open your mind and help those you care about to do the same. Why not take action? Wake yourself up and then wake others. Create! Why wait?

Do nothing for fame, glory or money. Strive to create a great change in humanity that will spread. This is noble universal service. We are sleeping giants. Baird Spalding in his book "The Life and Teachings of the Masters of the Far East" had this to say:

"The cycle is fast closing in which the blind of the whole race have led the blind into a welter of ignorance, superstition, and delusion created by those who believe as human beings think, rather than that which is true and real. The civilization that has risen on the delusions and superstitions of the closing centuries is submerging itself in the welter. Through the pain and tragedy of their misappropriated creations, a new race consciousness has been conceived and is fast evolving. In fact, the door is opening wide for its new birth." (Spaulding, 1924)

"Shine your Light and make a positive impact on the world; there is nothing so honorable as helping improve the lives of others." Roy T. Bennett

How do Light Beings Propel Themselves?
The amazing pictures on the right were taken by Grace Butler
Are they examples of Living Light propelling itself?

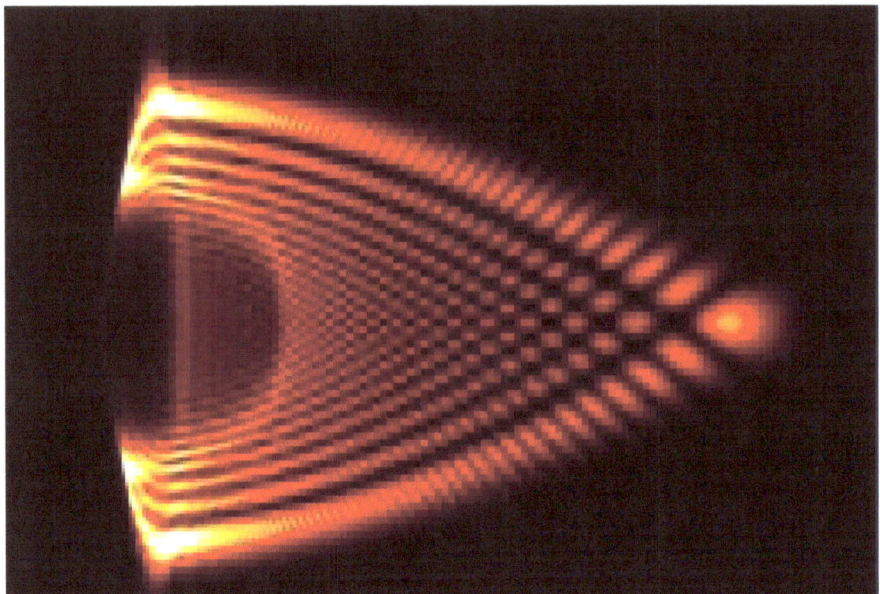

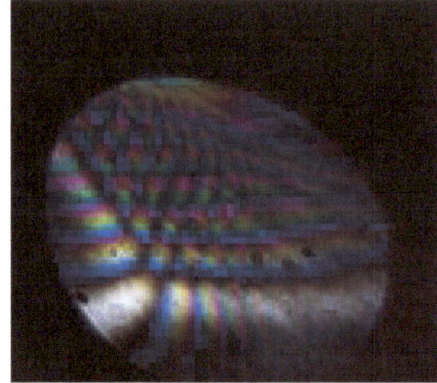

These images show the spatial distribution of charge for an accelerating wave packet, representing an electron. Brightest colors represent the highest charge levels. The self-acceleration of a particle predicted by this work is indistinguishable from acceleration that would be produced by a conventional electromagnetic field. (Chandler, 2015)

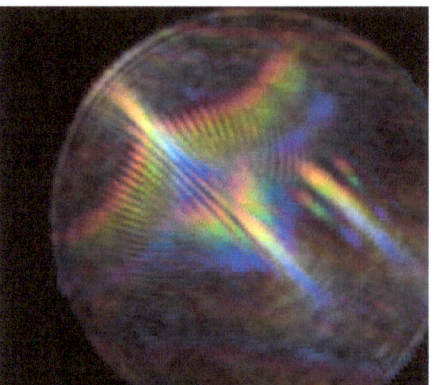

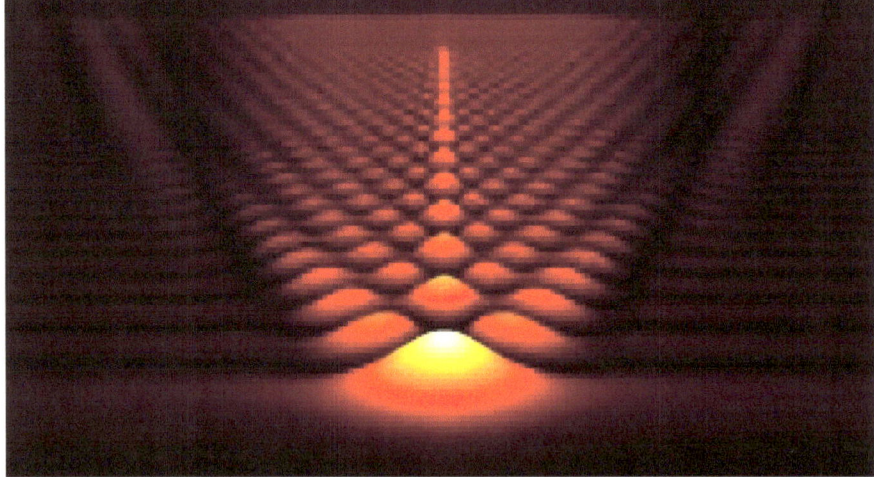

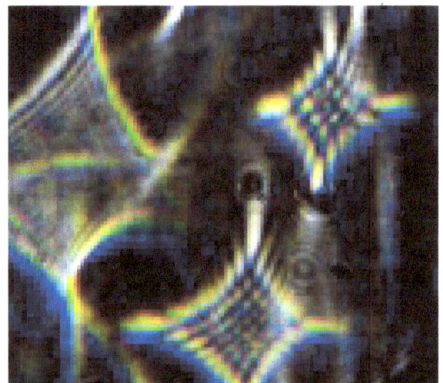

"Some physical principles have been considered immutable since the time of Isaac Newton: Light always travels in straight lines. No physical object can change its speed unless some outside force acts on it. Physicists at MIT have found that subatomic particles can be induced to speed up all by themselves, almost to the speed of light, without the application of any external forces". (Chandler, 2015)

Could the "outside force" acting on Light Beings be that on an electromagnetic field created by subtle energy? Is this similarity in appearance significant?

"The electron is gaining speed, getting faster and faster," Kaminer (a physist from MIT) says. "It looks impossible. You don't expect physics to allow this to happen." (Chandler, 2015)

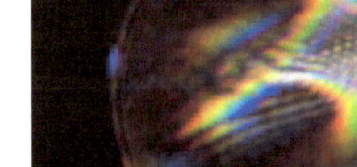

"The secret of health for both mind and body is not to mourn for the past, not to worry about the future, not to anticipate the future, but to live the present moment wisely and earnestly." Buddha

Are Light Beings Electrons?

Grace Butler took all these amazing pictures of Living Light. They all seem to be duplicating the propulsion pattern described on the previous page. Do these Light Beings behave as if they were propelling themselves like electrons? Perhaps they are!

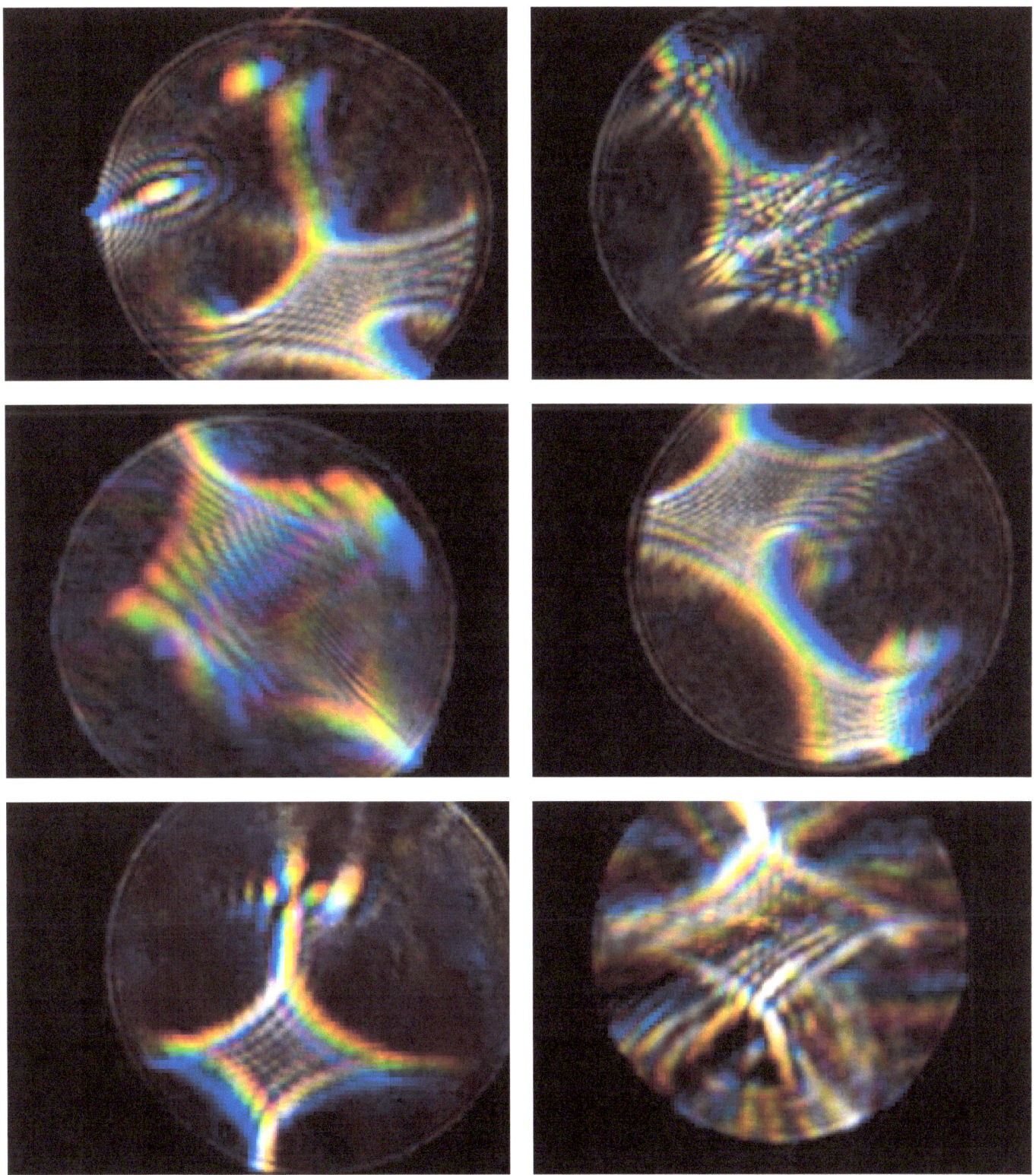

"When they shall know the Light of Me in them, then they shall be Me and I them." From The Divine Iliad - Walter Russell

The Unified Field Theory = The String Theory = The Theory of Everything

The Unified Field Theory, which John Hagelin, Ph.D., helped to develop, is identical to the "unified field of consciousness" posited by Maharishi Mahesh Yogi. It has been proposed that the unified field of modern theoretical physics and the field of "pure consciousness" are identical. The proposed relationship between consciousness and the unified field is consistent with all known physical principles, but requires an expanded physical framework for the understanding of consciousness. Is everything created out of consciousness?

The evolution of scientific knowledge often requires extending the domain of scientific research to include areas that were previously outside the range of scientific investigation. Many eminent physicists feel that the final and most important scientific frontier is consciousness. Currently, with the experiential technologies provided by Maharishi Vedic Science, consciousness is entering the realm of systematic, scientific investigation. The resulting science of consciousness suggests a profound and previously unsuspected unification of objective and subjective realms of experience. Vedic science might lead to a revolution in the field of scientific knowledge and methodology, and may constitute one of the key discoveries of our age. It could shift paradigms, and I believe it will.

String Theory states that all matter in the universe is composed of microscopic 1-dimensional strings. Furthermore, it states that "Strings" are tiny bits of pure energy (consciousness?) that are the smallest constituents of matter and force interaction in our universe. It also proposes that all universal constituents are defined by the vibrational mode of its string, similar to the vibrations of a guitar string. Steven S. Gubser, a physics professor at Princeton University, and author of *The Little Book of String Theory*, sums up the theory rather nicely, asserting that, "String theory aims to be a unifying picture, where each [particle] is a different vibrational mode of a string".

The Theory of Everything, with 26 dimensions, hypothesizes that there are objects with imaginary mass that could ruin the very physics of our universe. The notion that particles and forces are only excitations of vibrational modes—string theory, and all that it entails, is astonishing. Most of us only experience four dimensions (three of space and one of time). Some people are now exploring the fifth dimension. It is hard to imagine 26 dimensions.

Traditional string theories include two kinds of strings, open and closed. Those that are open generally have endpoints, which vary in length. Could the fan and line Light Being pictures by Grace Butler be visible examples of open strings? Closed strings, on the other hand, have no endpoints and are generally circular in nature. Could orbs be closed strings?

This is a very simple explanation of an extremely complex theory. If you would like to learn more about this theory, I recommend you do your homework. This is not a topic traditional media focuses on. The powers in power prefer it that way. Grace Butler took all of the pictures on the next several pages.

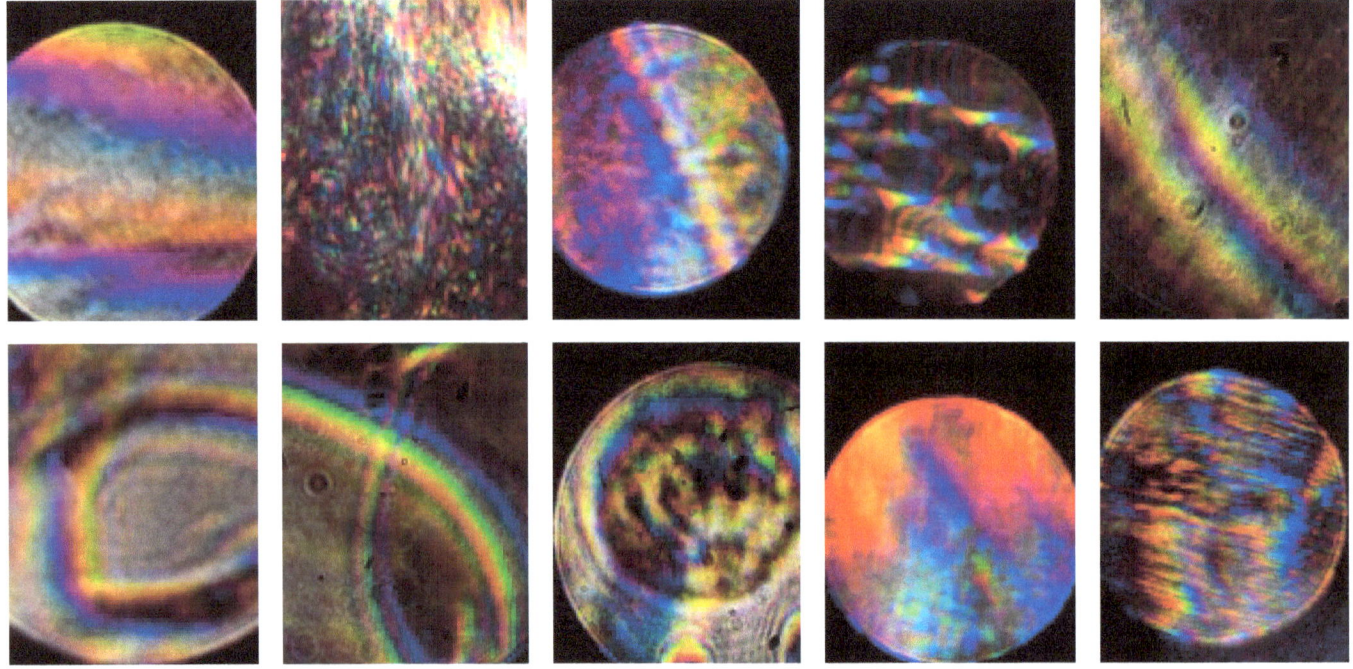

All knowledge exists. All mankind can have it for the asking. It is within man, awaiting his awareness of its all-presence. Walter Russell

Could these pictures, by Grace Butler, be illustrations of the Unified Field (String) Theory? I see a fairy, an elf and an angel in these.

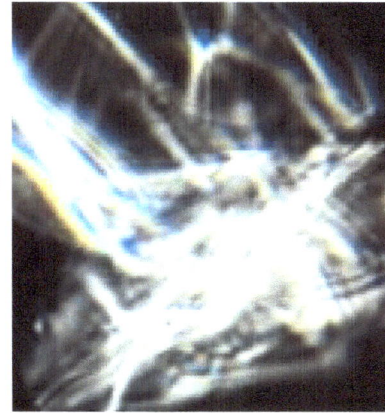 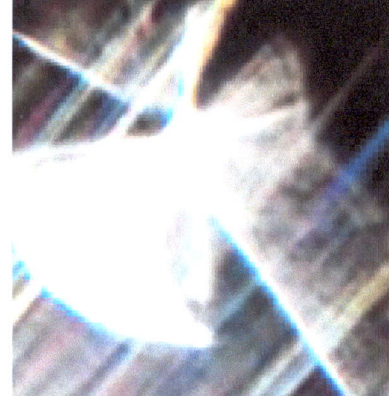 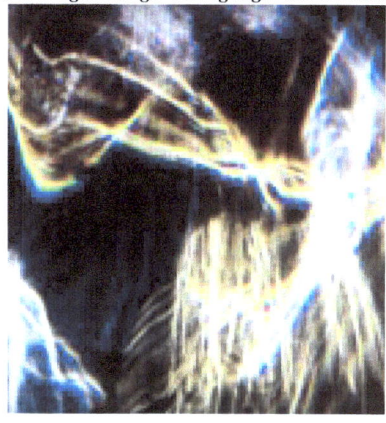

Light can do amazing things. I've never seen any pictures like these. I hope science investigates this phenomenon. Are these illustrations of the String Theory, or the Unified Field Theory of physics, in action? Are these visual representations of Alfvén waves, as defined in the section on plasma?

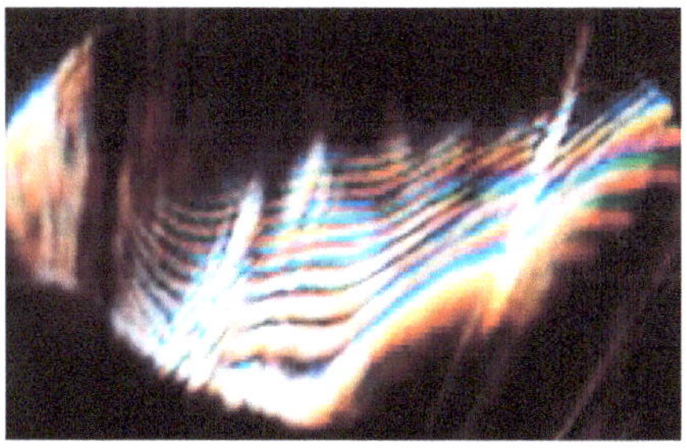

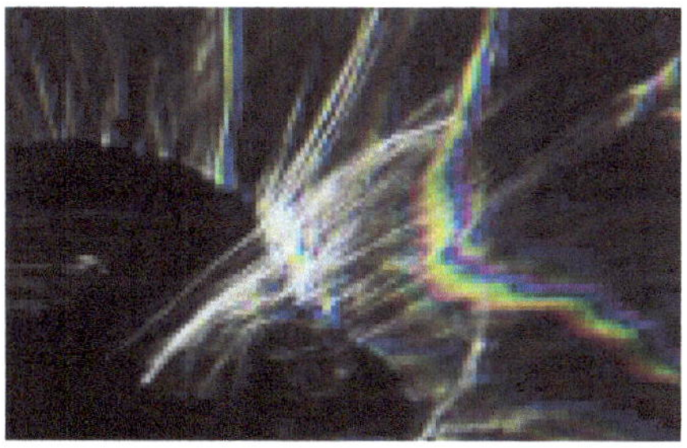

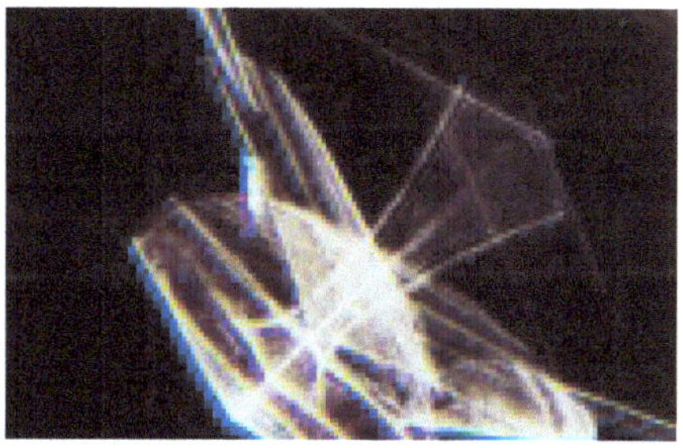

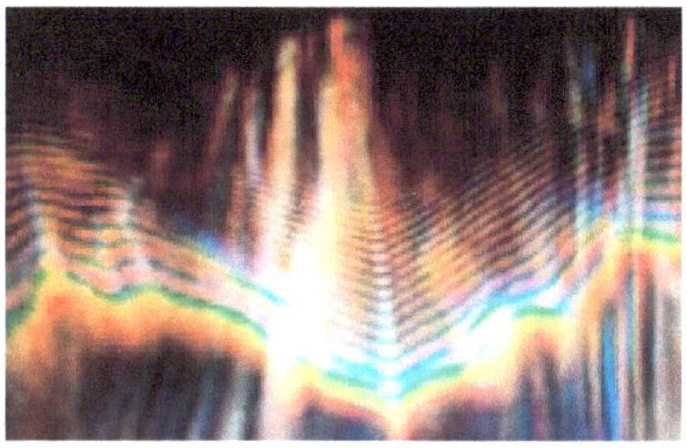

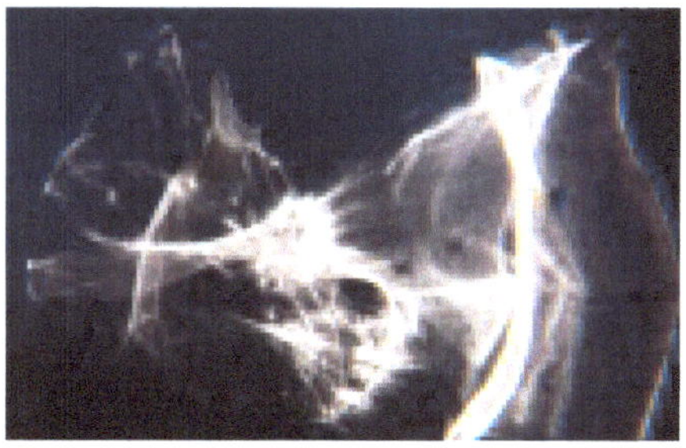

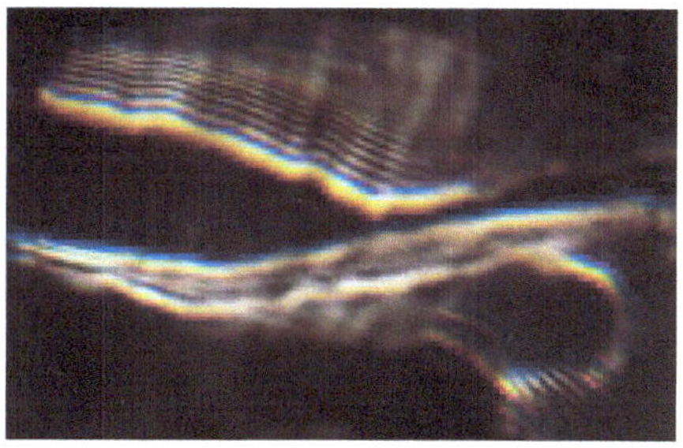

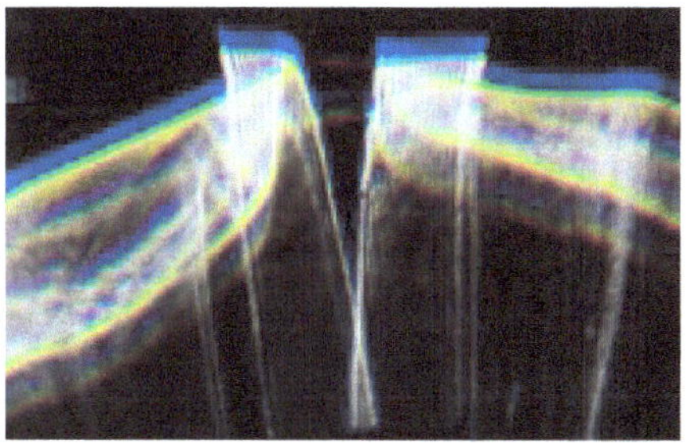

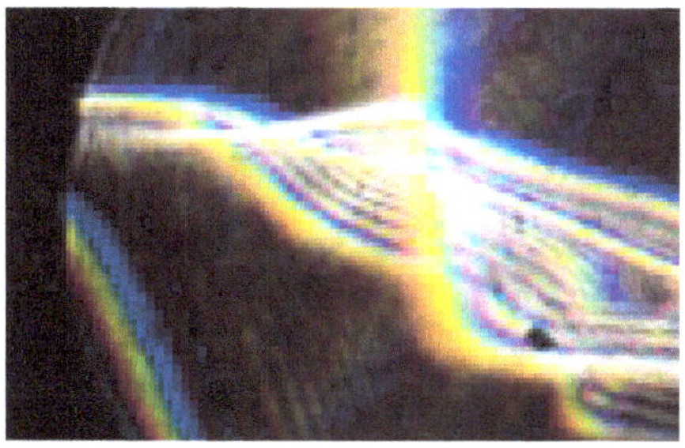

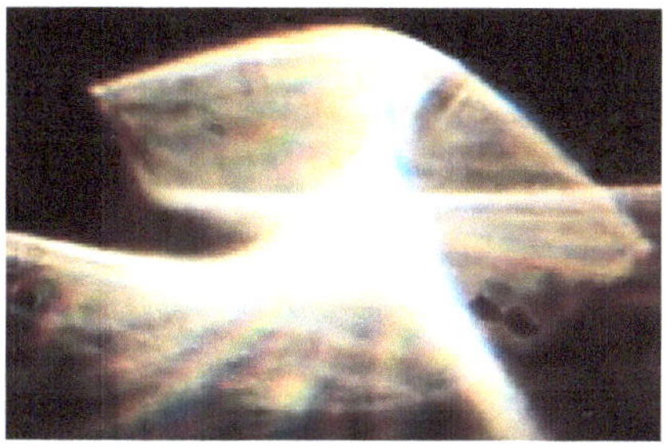

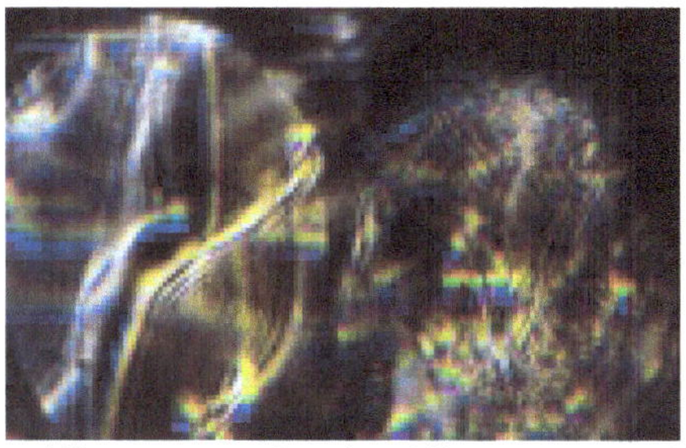

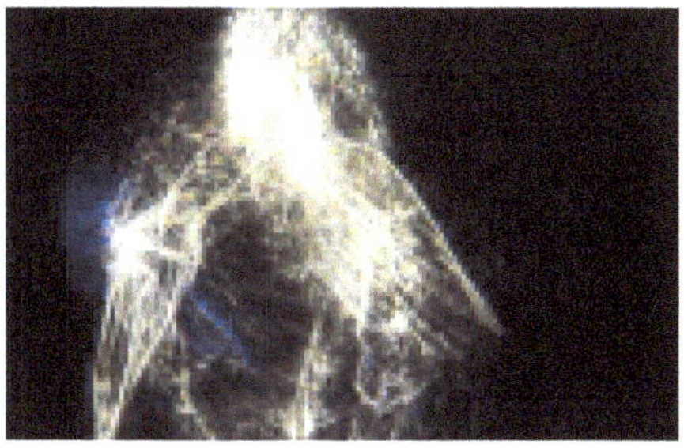

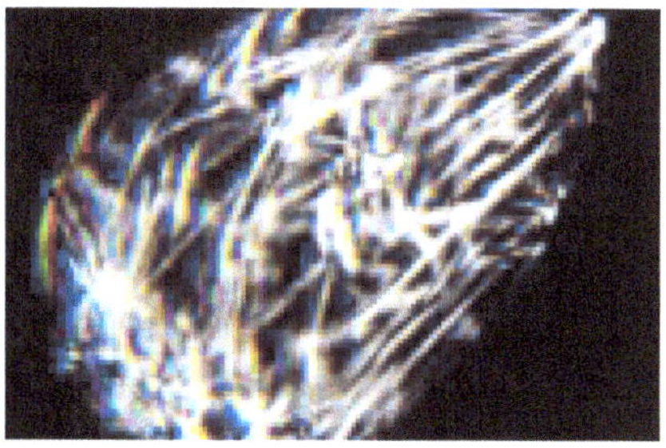

When one acquires the ability to connect with the Light within, everything observed and experienced through the five senses in the outer world takes on a new meaning, which releases the child within to want to relearn that which we already know. Norma Milanovich

These photos by Grace Butler seem to be "creatures." Are these the "critters" others have referred to? Is this how they multiply? Some look like jelly fish. Others look like worms. I don't have words to describe what others may be. What do you think? Dust on the lense? That idea is laughable.

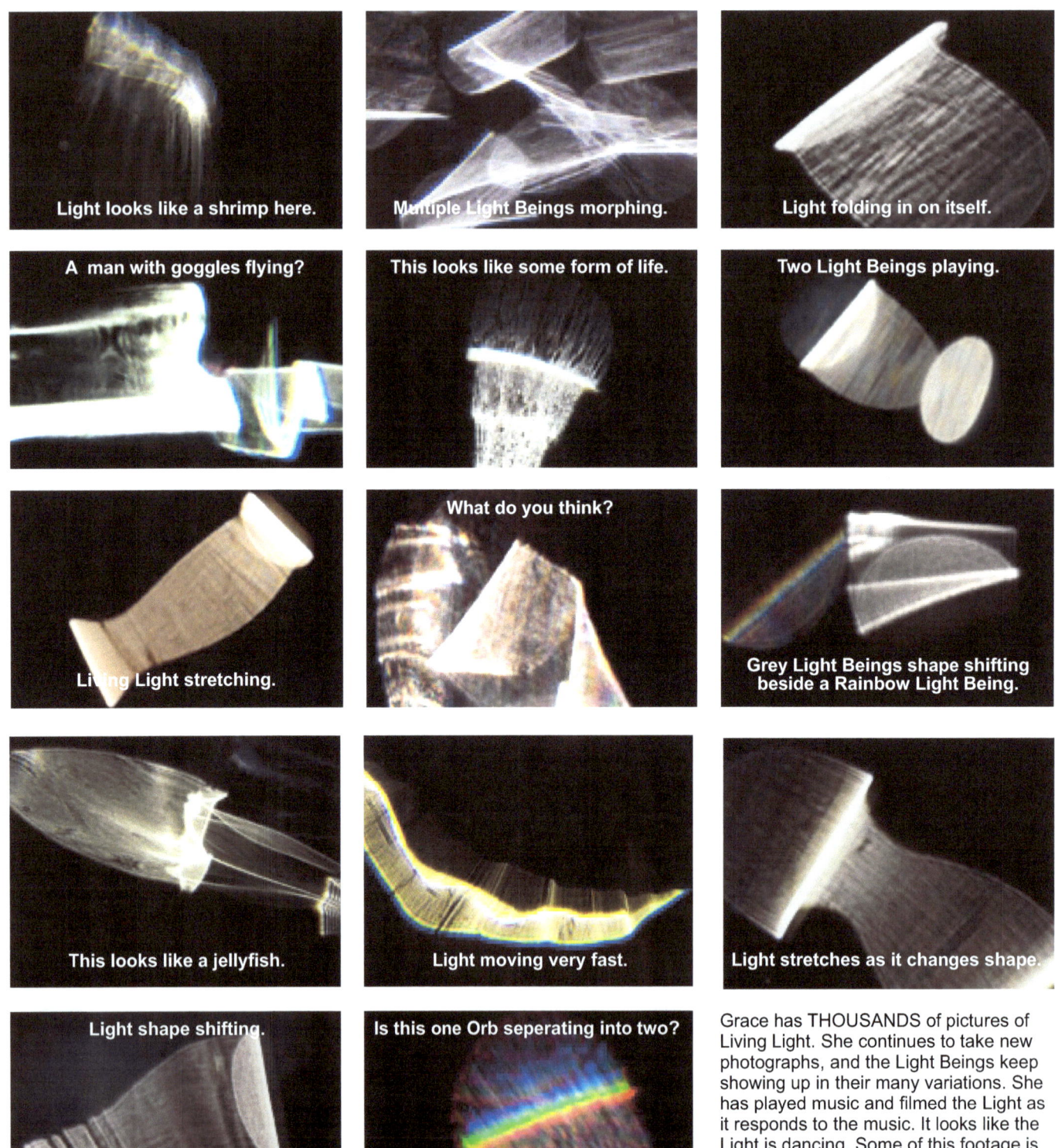

Light looks like a shrimp here.

Multiple Light Beings morphing.

Light folding in on itself.

A man with goggles flying?

This looks like some form of life.

Two Light Beings playing.

Living Light stretching.

What do you think?

Grey Light Beings shape shifting beside a Rainbow Light Being.

This looks like a jellyfish.

Light moving very fast.

Light stretches as it changes shape.

Light shape shifting.

Is this one Orb seperating into two?

Grace has THOUSANDS of pictures of Living Light. She continues to take new photographs, and the Light Beings keep showing up in their many variations. She has played music and filmed the Light as it responds to the music. It looks like the Light is dancing. Some of this footage is included in the documentary based on this book. Grace has taken video of Light dancing to the song Hello Dolly. This footage can be found on both our YouTube channels.

The curriculum of earth is to learn love and Light. Norma Milanovich

Light Beings can appear to fan out, as these photosby Grace illustrate. What causes the different variations in their expressions? This is a mystery. Isn't it time for some scientific investigation? Are these visual representations of Alfvén waves, as defined below? Are these examples of String Theory?

What is Plasma?

Plasma is the fourth state of matter, which is highest energy state of matter. The three other states of matter are solids, liquids and gases. Plasma makes up the sun and stars, and it is the most common state of matter in the universe. "99.9 percent of the Universe is made up of plasma," says Dr. Dennis Gallagher, a plasma physicist at NASA's Marshall Space Flight Center.

Plasma is a gas that has been energized to the point that some of the electrons break free from, but travel with, their nucleus. To produce and maintain the highly energetic state that exists within plasma, there must be a continual supply of energy. Could this energy be subtle energy (life-force energy)?

Like gases, plasmas have no fixed shape or volume and can flow like a liquid or can contain areas that are like clumps of atoms sticking together. Plasma has the ability to act as a whole rather than as separate atoms. It behaves differently from a gas and has what scientists call collective behavior. Being made of charged particles, plasmas can do things gases cannot, like conduct electricity. Plasma is more readily influenced by electric and magnetic fields than by gravity. The motion of electrons and ions in plasma produces its own electric and magnetic fields, and electromagnetic radiation.

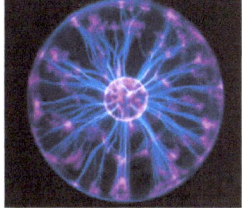

A ball of plama.

Particles in plasma can interact via electricity and magnetism, and they can do so at far greater distances than an ordinary gas. That in turn means waves become more important when discussing what goes on in plasma. One such wave is called an Alfvén wave. An Alfvén wave happens when the magnetic field in plasma is disturbed, creating a wave that travels along the field lines. Some of the "fan" type Light Beings Grace has photographed may be visual representation of Alfvén waves.

Plasma Beings

"There are many different sentient forms or advanced consciousness life forms that exist in states that are vastly unfamiliar to us on the Earth. On Earth, we tend to associate intelligent life with some kind of physical body or form that we can see. However, some of the most advanced levels of interdimensional Light Beings, that have the highest states of multidimensional consciousness in the Universe, exist in formless and bodiless states as Plasma Beings. Plasma Beings are made up of the God Source power supply, and are immensely loving and compassionate. They are capable of projecting their consciousness throughout multiple dimensions simultaneously. They may travel vast intergalactic distances in plasma orb bodies, and they are most commonly seen in these temporary bodies, which may appear as biological plasma ships. Some Plasma Beings are massive Stars or can be comprised of entire interstellar systems that make up a certain species. Many of the Guardians that are hosting planet earth's Ascension Cycle, are massive Plasma Beings or Suns. They know firsthand that connecting into the Universal plasma source and embodying plasma light is the key to spiritual freedom and ascending into higher consciousness states. Thus, many Plasma Beings have returned to the earth or are revealing themselves to us now. They are here to help humanity learn about the Ascension and the importance of plasma to build our light body. Plasma light helps us to attain higher consciousness states when we commune with the universal forces of unconditional love and peace." (http://ascensionglossary.com/index.php/Plasma_Beings)

As Above, So Below
Grace Butler
(Inspired by messages from Norma Milanovich)

In our physical world we have energy, light, vibration, and motion. These things exist in the etheric world as well. The spiritual and the etheric worlds correspond with one another. Science often looks only at parts of systems, so they are unaware of interconnections and relationships of phenomena.

We will understand consciousness better upon the premise that mind gives rise to matter. The basic energy of the universe is consciousness, also called the Golden Liquid Light, God Force, Life Force…the list goes on. It is our own individual unique consciousness, our essence that expands as we grow spiritually. Eventually we will become one with the ALL.

To understand better, consider that our world is holographic. Holographic means that contained within each small part of the whole is the whole itself. A hologram projects a three-dimensional image, which shows various views, and images depending on our perspective.

Our consciousness defines our unique characteristics and is the basis of our essence. We impose an order of regularity on our world by the way we perceive the world which will be consistent with our expectations, beliefs, and past experiences. Therefore, we create our own experiences.

There is nothing in the universe, which exist separately, or in isolation. Therefore what we do, say and believe affects everything everywhere. Every cell within us contains intelligence.

There exists a basic wisdom and knowledge within the universe, which is beyond our physical reality. As more expand their consciousness, and live honoring their responsibility to themselves and others, Earth will approach the Fifth Dimension.

It's time for us to understand our connection to others. As people choose to live by this understanding, it will expand us to a higher spiritual consciousness. As we grow in consciousness we will realize that we are part of a whole. We are all One. All planes of existence exist simultaneously and in this synchronicity, all is in motion.

The principle of "As above, so below; as below, so above" means that we will have Heaven on Earth. This will happen when enough souls are aligned with Heaven by learning to live in harmony and agreement with the All, the Oneness.

"As above, so below; as below, so above" must be understood as existing in three planes. These three planes are the physical, the mental, and the spiritual planes. There must be harmony or agreement with the All and this idea is critical. There are many elements that exist on these three planes and not one of them can step outside the One, so it is most necessary that all are truly in harmony, one to another.

People are not limited to what they can see and experience. We only seem to be separated from the larger picture of the Macrocosm. Agreements have been made in Universal Mind that are in harmony with Divine Law. Universal Mind is a force field and we are here to understand this. We are becoming co-creators with this force field. We, as humans, must not see ourselves as separate. We are connected.

We have allowed the physical world to hold us in a state of unconsciousness. We are sleeping giants. Many are asleep, quiet and subdued and have forgotten who they are. When all awaken and connect, we will achieve great things, magnificent things.

Consciousness holds us together. We live in a pulsating, vibrating field of Liquid Light and endless energy. We are here to connect the physical plane with the mental and spiritual ones. When we do this we will have the power to affect any and all things in any moment of time. The only reason we are not already powerful is that most have not understood this concept and have not known that we can do magnificent things. Our minds will be connected with Universal Mind and be strengthened by discipline and willpower. We must stop entertaining our five senses and focus our attention on going within. There we will connect our mind to other planes and dimensions of reality and with the All. All power is then returned to us, our journey ends with the awakening and we will learn how to access other realms.

This physical world vibrates at the lowest vibrational rate, while the plane of Spirit vibrates at the highest.

All vibrations are contained within the All. There are infinite variations within Universal Mind. Any positive change of condition in one variation can uplift them all because all planes of existence are affecting all others. All occur simultaneously. This means we must watch our thoughts, words, emotions, and actions. Decisions humans make affect the celestial realms and the angelic, devic and elemental kingdoms, since all are interconnected.

As we begin to realize this truth, the world will take on a new meaning. The power within our mind and hearts will begin to grow. We are destined to transform the world by increasing our individual Light frequencies. We will increase our Light frequencies through the power of our inner journey and that of our mind.

Light is the highest vibrational frequency known to humanity. Spirit is Light accelerated, and matter is light slowed down. We must learn to live more in the cosmic light of Spirit, and less in the physical world of illusion. Humanity has no time to wait. The time is NOW. We can build Heaven on Earth.

Grace Butler shares an excerpt from Walter Russell's book, *"The Secret of Light"*:

"Within the secret of Light is the answer to all of these heretofore unanswered questions, and many more, which the ages have not yet solved. This revelation of the nature of Light will be the inheritance of man in this coming New Age of greater comprehension. Its unfoldment will prove the existence of God by methods and standards acceptable to science and religion alike. It will lay spiritual foundation under the present material one of science.

The two greatest elements in civilization, religion and science, will thus find unity in the marriage of the two. Likewise human relationships will become more balanced because of greater knowledge of universal law, which lies behind all of the processes which light uses to interweave the patterned forms of this electric wave universe.

There is no department of life which will not be vitally affected by this new knowledge of the nature of Light, from the university to the laboratory, from government to industry, and from nation to nation.

I therefore give it to you with all of its clarity as I myself have become aware of it from behind the scenes of this cosmic cinema of light illusion which is our universe." Walter Russell (Russell, 1947)

Amazing Living Light pictures taken by Grace Butler with a digital camera without flash. I thought my rainbow Light Beings were bright and inspiring. Then I met Grace, saw her photography, and realized there is much more to this strange light than I had ever imagined. All of the pictures on the following pages are ones she took.

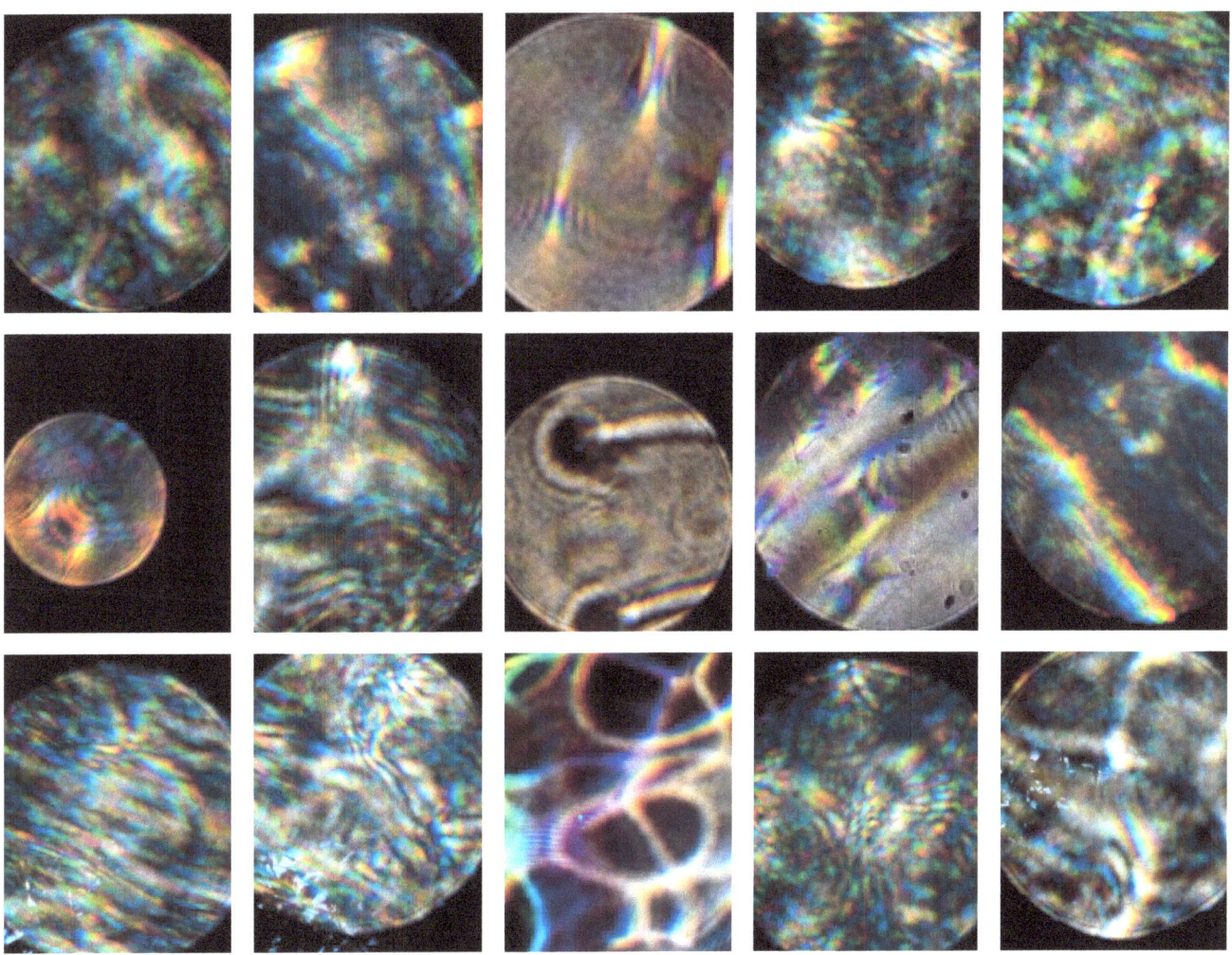

Norma Manilovich received the following information by channeling the Arcturians. Channeling is a means of communicating with any consciousness that is not in human form by allowing that consciousness to express itself through the channel. The Arcturians are a loving and caring species of extraterrestrials who rank the highest in our galaxy. They protect us from vile alien species and boost our vibration. This is what the Arcturians recently had to say:

This transformation into the New Age was described once, by the Arcturians, as the birthing of a planet (Earth) into a star in the Heavens. They said that it has been written since Babylon that the Earth would journey into the Age of Aquarius and become a Garden of Eden in the universe. They also explained that this event was happening because of the precession of the equinoxes, and that earth's position in this universal parade of stars was guided by forces higher than we can imagine.

They say that the world is a microcosm of the universe which is our macrocosm. They say that all is energy and that energy is Light. Out of Light energy came sound energy in the original creation. Out of Light and sound comes the formation of all that is. Each object, whether solid, liquid, or gas, has its own code, which is a vibratory frequency. This vibration is created out of Light. Since humans contain a consciousness that can be controlled, and since consciousness is thought, then each individual is actually a co-creator with the Divine.

The Arcturians described this whole phenomenon as a scientific one. They stated that our physicists were already beginning to make connections among these principles and concepts and soon would be able to document the concept of Oneness, which is a part of the millennium which we are entering.

The universe in which you reside is magical and powerful. It is the totality of universal consciousness and is mind energy. It is also perfect. It contains the sum of all that was and ever will be for your existence while you reside within it. It is the macrocosm of which you are the microcosm. Therefore, your intellect, which is a part of this universal consciousness, has no boundaries. You are one part of the total sum of all there is. - The Arcturians

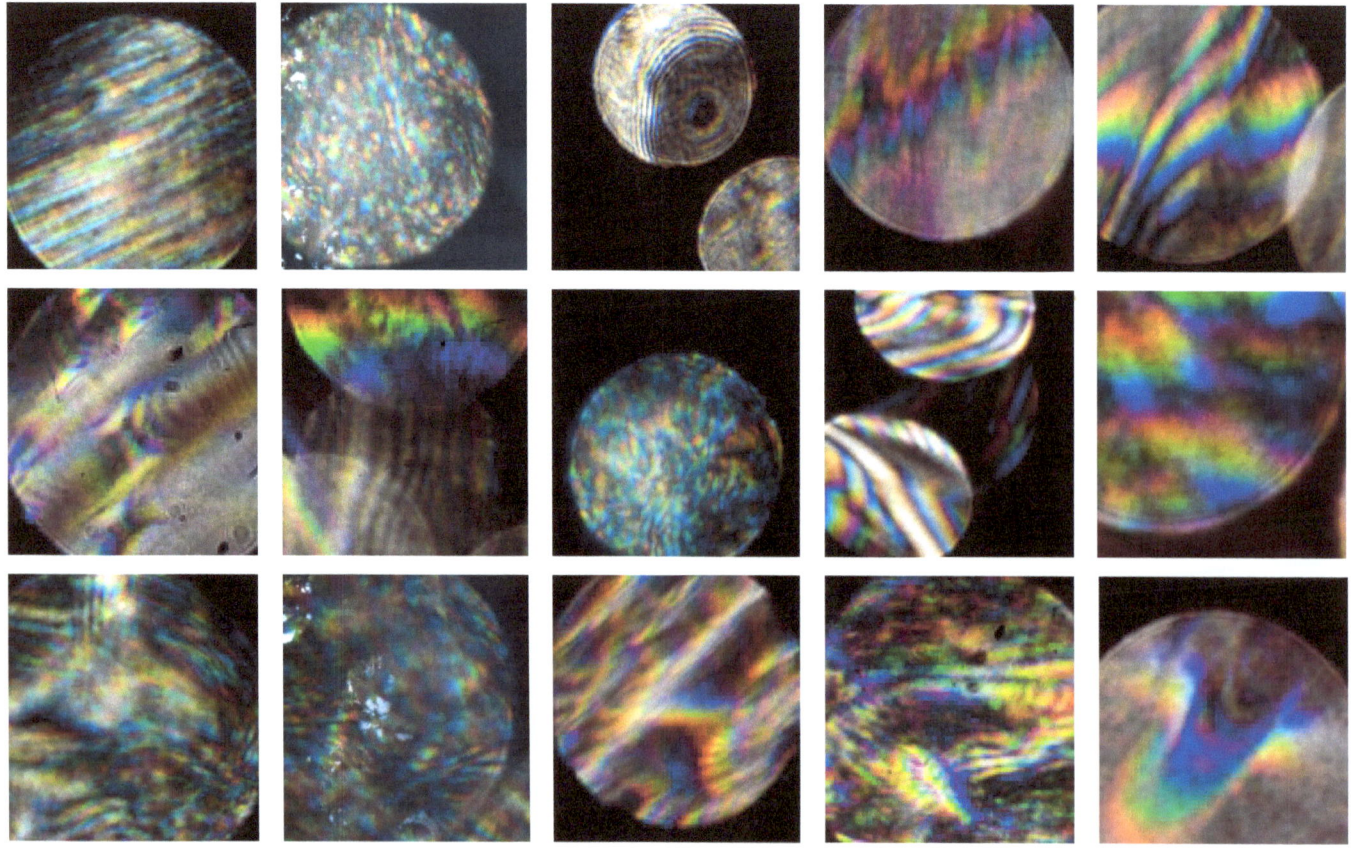

Intellect is freedom and the courage to explore areas where others dare not go.

The Power of Love

Recently Grace received another form of communication. This time it was in writing. She was deleting files from her computer that she no longer used or needed. She found a file she had titled, but had never added any content to. The name of the file was "The Power of Love". This was an empty file that had been titled but held no content. Content mysteriously appeared in her previously empty file containing a message for her. She believes a spiritual entity or group of spiritual beings had reached her and added text to her empty file. She had been questioning Spirit for a very long time. Her answer appeared in a very unique way. The message below has not been edited:

I want to say right away that I am willing to get into this only because you have expressed an interest in doing it. I have no agenda but Love for you and for all of that which is created. I am not a being who has time for taking little trips of fantasy into other realms for the fun of it. I am serious and I wish that to be known. I have little concern for those who believe not nor for those who wish to start a new religion of me. I will shut down quickly if I see that occurring.

Grace, you are a very good person and you do not even know it yet. I see you judge yourself as though you were not any good; only maybe just a little bit good. I am telling you that we need more like you and if we can accomplish this, all will be healed that is going wrong. I am going to give you a letter of a sorts in which you can address those scientists who would say that the orbs you take pictures of are nothing more than some kind of easily explained phenomena.

I am going to ask them to consider how you are able to see light in the process of bonding itself into the curved lined balls. What the curved lined balls are is a process in which matter is being put together. It will manifest for you in due time. It will be all that you want it to be and if you are not sure what you want, it knows for you that you want something you have asked for many times.

It is that which you asked for that is both silver and gold and fruit. It will be accomplished in time and you will have it for evidence to use it for an example. It will be good to see for you doubt a lot and we want you to cease from doubting. I know that is hard to do but with the help we will provide, you will be able to do it. To erase all doubt is always the hardest kind of thing for people to do. It requires one to deny what is and to relax and know and appreciate.

It is just that for us to begin to give to you the words that you seem to want is not easy for us because we don't know what you want to understand.

Now, let's talk about time. It is a construct, as you know it to be. God, or All That Is, uses time as a way of playing out parts of himself. All the dramas you are presented with are themes to test and serve to grow you into a better person.

It is going to be constructed a little differently from a point in time, which is fast approaching. It will be no longer a long wait until what you believe to be true, comes into existence. It is already working that way for many, to a certain degree. It will increase and you will walk in such a state of grace that you will find life to be so pleasant that you are not ever dissatisfied.

These words are etched into her memory. She finds herself believing more every day that what was communicated in this message will manifest.

The object referred to in the message as being "silver and gold and fruit" was a fanciful idea she used to think about. She never told anyone that she wished for a miracle that would manifest something similar. She often thought that if one can bring something out of the etheric, then she was going to stick to one thing to manifest. She hoped to manifest a silver platter filled with apples, made of pure gold. She thought of this often, but never believed it was truly possible. Now she firmly believes that it is possible and will come to pass.

Grace says it's time for all of us to believe in miracles. Miracles are something everyone can manifest. We can create them when we know we have the power to create them.

Grace has read many books about miracles. She considers seeing orbs appear in so many places by so many people a modern miracle. She thinks the Light Beings in her photographs are here to help us awaken to our own powers. The power of our thought is greater than any agent of evil operating in our world. People will learn to understand how powerful thoughts are in the near future.

To see more of Graces' photography, and hear some of her favorite readings, visit her YouTube channel (Grace Butler) at https://www.youtube.com/user/TheDoveLady

"When I said 'I am the way, the truth and the life,' I did not intend to convey the thought to mankind that I, Myself, was the only true Light." Jesus

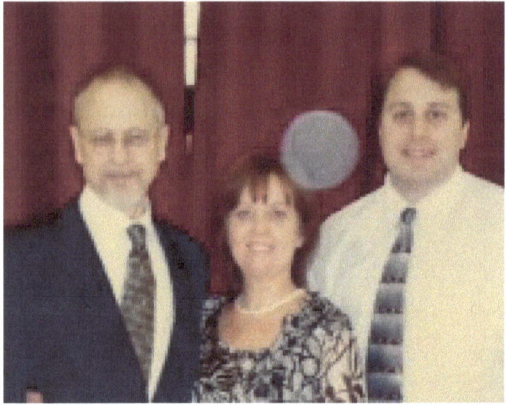

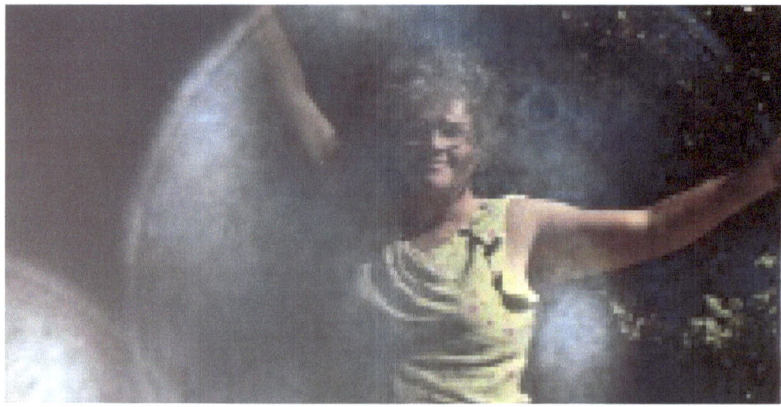

A friend of Grace Butlers' from the internet sent her this picture. Her friends wanted her father to be there with her for his funeral. They invited him to join them, even though he was no longer alive. I believe her father is above and in front of her. He showed up as an Orb in the picture to let her know he was there.

While in the Ozark Mountains with her sister, Grace saw orbs in her camera's view finder. The orbs were all around her sister, Maggie. Grace asked Maggie to step over to another spot so that the Orb would be in line with her. If it had been a smaller Orb, she might have ask her to hold out her hand to a certain spot so it would look as if she were holding the Orb. This is how Grace got the shots of her brother-in-law and Gerald "holding" Orbs.

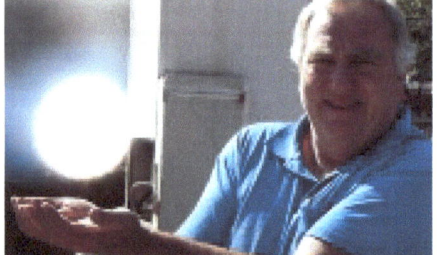

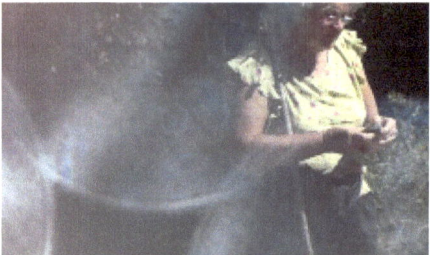

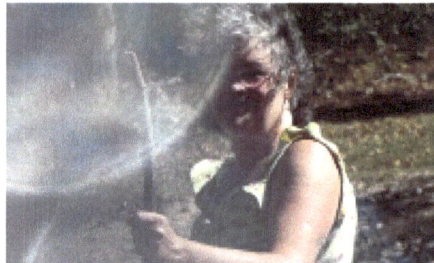

Grace told her brother-in-law to hold out his hands as she took this picture. A beautiful Orb joins the fun!

Gerald Bringle is shown in the pictures below. He took the beautiful shot at the upper left corner of this collection. He is the only person who has been able to duplicate the technique Grace uses to photograph Light Beings. I was able to photograph grey Orbs using her technique, but have not been able to duplicate any of her other photos of Light Beings…yet!

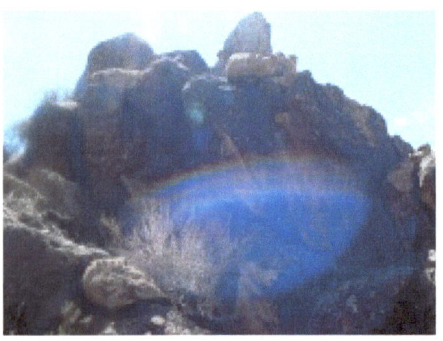

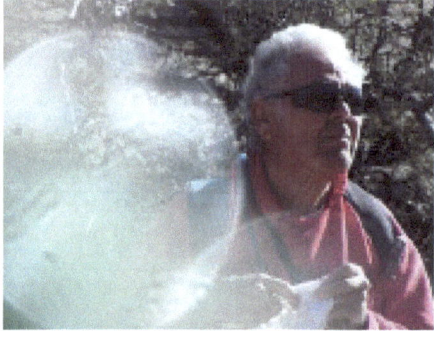

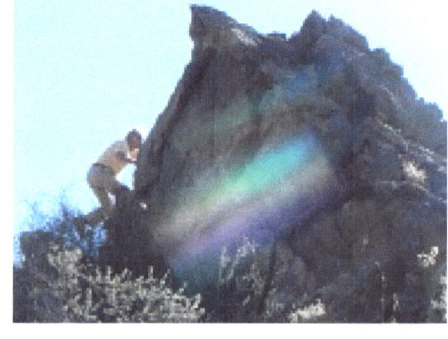

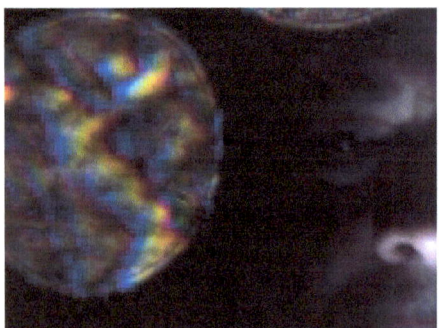

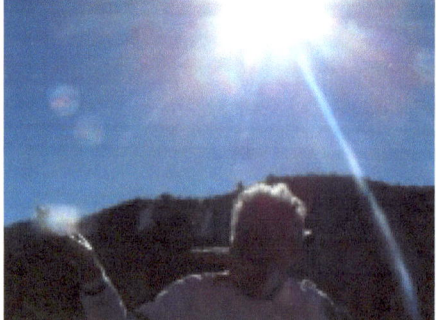

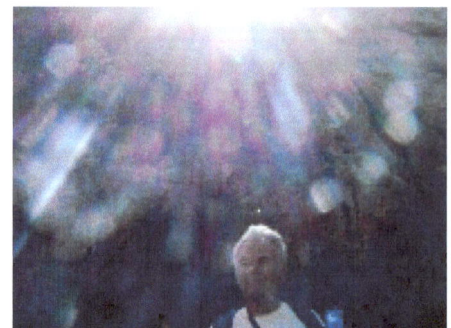

We actors of the play must, therefore, be content with the lines of the play revealed to each of us in Light. We must, likewise, be ever joyous at our continuous transformation, as each one of us learns our part, line by line, the better to fulfill it worthily. Walter Russell

The evidence presented here will hopefully lead to research and investigation into this phenomenon. Many scientists are, unfortunately, stuck in an outdated paradigm. "Yes, the world is flat, so don't confuse us with the facts" they have said in the past. They have their minds made up. It's time to expand our understanding of this phenomenon. Understanding may come from a new science and a new type of physics. I hope scientists will welcome an opportunity for advancement into uncharted territories.

The powers that be, to maintain their power, may be intentionally blocking the release of new information. Perhaps they don't want the public to know. I'm relatively certain that they are not interested in educating people about the different types of life that exist. They probably prefer to maintain their paradigm of power, controlling what the public is "allowed" to know. They are masters of disinformation. How many types of life do they know about? Do they know more than they will admit?

I think it's time we expand our current understanding of physics, and question the current scientific paradigm. The powers that be, to maintain their power, may be intentionally blocking the release of new information. Perhaps they don't want the public to know that there is more to life than they've been taught to believe.

"If I was to favor one of these notions, it would be the lights-as-creatures possibility…that earth lights are, in fact, energy forms produced by processes at the very limits of our current scientific comprehension. I think we are looking at an energy manifestation that is either an unfamiliar form of electromagnetism, or else it is of a completely unknown order that interacts, resonates, in some way with parts of the electromagnetic spectrum. Such a secret force has long been assumed by traditional societies. In old China it was called Chi; to the Australian aborigines it is kurunba: a primary sea of force that underpins the manifestation of energy effects and matter in the material world. Either way, the road to its comprehension will have to be through an extended form of geophysics. This energy has remarkable characteristics and has much to teach us." (Devereux, 1989)

"With these moving balls of light, we are clearly approaching areas of phenomena that suggest more complex physics than simple discharge mechanisms." (Devereux, 1989) A discharge mechanism refers to light discharged by the friction of crystals rubbing together. Geophysics may partially explain a form of light, but is it intelligent or conscious? I believe that there are more complex types of physics involved, which hopefully will be investigated.

We are the ones we've been waiting for. Be the change you wish to see in the world. If not us, who? If not now, when? Humanity is running out of time. We must pull our heads out of the sand and educate ourselves about the power of our collective consciousness. We can prevent the power elite from destroying civilization as we know it, but we must take action now. The sand is slipping through the hourglass. It's one minute before midnight. United, humanity can expose the elite cowards and regain our birthrights. We are born with the right to life, liberty and the pursuit of happiness. It's time to legalize freedom for the entire human race. How dare those in power play with the planet and all life on it, as if they owned it. The power elite have no right to destroy our beautiful home and us along with it. We cannot fight fire with fire, and have no desire to do so. Love will rule the day and there is hope for us all. Theirs is a rigged game. It will backfire on them and they will be exposed. United we stand, divided they win. They won't. Our future is bright. Fear not. Our combined Light will always, and in all ways, prevail. We have infinite assistance from the unseen spiritual world.

Awareness is the key to change. Once we become aware of anything different, we can seek to understand it. This search expands our consciousness as our awareness increases. There is something communicating with us. Now that we know, our perceptions may, or may not, change.

Open your mind and learn new things. Educate yourself by reading books. Don't rely on mainstream media or traditional educational institutions. We can all learn from messengers and visionaries who have paved the way.

Only the beginning......

References

Aldone, M. (n.d.). (2014). *Strange Artifacts Reveal History of Human Origins is Wrong.* Retrieved March 08, 2018, from https://www.apparentlyapparel.com/news/strange-artifacts-reveal-history-of-human-origin-is-wrong Article based on source: *Grooved Sphere from South Africa, 2.8 Billion Years Old by Colin Andrews*

Authors, Multiple. (1996). *Ufology: a Scientific Enigma: MUFON 1996 International UFO Symposium Proceedings: Twenty-Seventh Annual MUFON UFO Symposium.* Seguin, TX: Mutual UFO Network.

Brennan, B. A. (1987). *Hands Of Light.* New York: Bantam Books.

Broom, D. (n.d.). Bioelectrography and Bioenergetic Cancer Screening: New Dimensions In Imaging Techniques. Retrieved March 08, 2018, from https://www.canceractive.com/cancer-active-page-link.aspx?n=1519

Chandler, D. Ph.D., Massachusetts Institute of Technology, (2015, January 21). *New Analysis Shows A Way To Self-Propel Subatomic Particles.* Retrieved March 08, 2018, from https://phys.org/news/2015-01-analysis-self-propel-subatomic-particles.html#jCp.

Goode, C. (2018, January 08). *Cosmic Disclosure- Guide to Non-Terrestrial Beings - Corey Goode.* Retrieved March 08, 2018, from https://www.youtube.com/watch?v=ZXLP5Q-WdR4 Sphere Being Alliance

Goode, C. (n.d.*). Sphere Being Alliance Website.* Retrieved March 08, 2018, from https://www.sphere-beingalliance.com/

Cooper, D., & Crosswell, K. (2008). *Enlightenment Through Orbs.* Scotland, UK: Findhorn Press.

Cremo, M. A., & Thompson, R. L. (1993). *Forbidden Archeology: The Hidden History Of The Human Race.* Los Angeles: Bhaktivedanta Institute. *Grooved Sphere From South Africa, 2.8 Billion Years Old. Colin Andrews (http://www.colinandrews.net/ForbiddenArcheologys)*

Devaney, J. *Is Sacred Geometry a Key for Enlightenment? Uplift*, J. Devaney, 17 July 2016, upliftconnect.com/sacred-geometry-enlightenment/.

Devereux, P. (1989). *Earth Lights Revelation: UFOs and Mystery Lightform Phenomena:The Earths Secret Energy Force.* London: Blandford.

G. (2011). *King James Study Bible: King James Version, Chestnut.* Place of publication not identified: Thomas Nelson.

Gemstone, T. (2018, February 13). *Daily Tarot February* 14, 2018 *Happy Valentine's Day!* Retrieved March 08, 2018, from https://www.youtube.com/watch?v=rcw7aLHbfdg
Viewer engagement: Timeline 00:20-00:29

Gemstone, T. (2018, January 19). Gemstone Tarot. Retrieved March 08, 2018, from https://www.youtube.com/channel/UCd4ea_m9DgzSHYHC-7VZQkQ.

Gilbert, P. R. (n.d.). The Hidden Energy Science of Sacred Geometry. Retrieved March 08, 2018, from https://vesica.org/sacred-geometry-articles/the-hidden-energy-science-of-sacred-geometry-2 Publisher Vesica Institute for Holistic Studies

God, 1. (1944). *The Open Bible.* London: Independent Press.

God, 1. (2011). *The Bible: American Standard Version.* Irvine, CA: Magnanimous Enterprises.

Heinemann, K. W., Ph.D. & Ledwith, M. (2010). *Orbs: Their Mission and Messages of Hope* (1st ed.). Carlsbad, CA: Hay House, Inc.
Inarritu, A. G. (Director). (2016). (2015). Revenant [Motion picture on DVD]. Milano: 20th Century Fox.

J., & P. (n.d.). *Invisible Life Force - A List of Choices.* Retrieved January 30, 2018, from http://www.higherawareness.com/manifesting-abundance/life-force-energy.html

Moorhouse, J. (Director). (2015, October 29). *The Dressmaker* [Video file]. Retrieved from https://www.amazon.com/dp/B01L9Q577Y?ref=nav_custrec_signin&tag=dv_dev_imdb_pcqcbwn32DM-20&. Moving Light Beings

Rawles, B. (2018). *Sacred Geometry Introductory Tutorial. The Geometry Code,*

Retrieved from https://www.geometrycode.com/sacred-geometry/
Robson, J., & Robson, P. (n.d.). *Invisible Life Force - A List of Choices.* Retrieved January 31, 2018, from http://www.higherawareness.com/manifesting-abundance/life-force-energy.html

Ross, G. (2016). Free State of Jones [Motion picture on DVD]. USA: Universal Pictures Home Entertainment.

Russell, W. (1994). *The Secret of Light* (1st ed.). University of Science & Philosophy.
revised (2018, January 25). The Secret of Light. 1st Edition 1947, 3rd Edition 1994 ISBN ISBN 1-879605-44-9

Sereda, D. (June 18, 2011*) Analysis Of NASA UFO*.flv Retrieved March 08, 2018, https://www.youtube.com/watch?v=Ta1P5Q0UnBQ&t=5s

Sheyer, C. (Director). (1994*). I Love Trouble* [Motion picture on DVD]. USA: Touchstone Pictures, Buena Vista Pictures.

Shimosawa, S. (Director). (2016). *Misconduct* [Motion picture on DVD]. USA: Mike and Marty Productions, Grindstone Entertainment Group, Lionsgate.

Spalding, B. (1924). *The Life and Teachings of the Masters of the Far East* (Revised ed., Six Books). Published: Self. ISBN-13: 978-0875165387 ISBN-10: 0875165389 Original 1924, Revised 2010.

Steiger, B. (2001). *Shadow World: Spiritual Encounters That Can Change your Life.* Mass Market Paperback.

Swanson, C., Ph.D. (2003). *The Synchronized Universe: New Science of the Paranormal.* Tucson, AZ: Poseidia Press. ISBN 0-9745261-0-X

Swanson, C., Ph.D. (2011). *LIFE FORCE: The Scientific Basis: Breakthrough Physics of Energy Medicine, Healing, Chi and Quantum Consciousness*. Tucson, AZ: Poseidia Press. ISBN 978-0-9745261-4-0

Sweet, L., Ph.D. (2005). *How To Photograph The Paranormal*. Charlottesville, VA: Hampton Roads Pub. Co.

T. (2014, January 31). *The Flower Of Life: Sacred Geometry Secret Of The Flower Of Life Truth!* Retrieved February 05, 2018, from https://www.youtube.com/watch?v=e3tcxY2aEzU

T. (2018, February 13). *Your Daily Focus for February 14*, 2018. Retrieved March 08, 2018, from https://www.youtube.com/watch?v=0ib81SGMEQw.

T. G (2017, July 19). *Daily Tarot Reading July* 20, 2017 *All Zodiac Signs*. Retrieved March 08, 2018, from https://www.youtube.com/watch?v=4AEBVmd_yrw. Gemstone Tarot. Subject: Tribe Card and "Come to Mama" (Times of appearance on video timeline: 2:09-2:10: - Rectangular Light Being travels from the mantle on the left side to the top of her head. 3:55-3:57: - A quick bright Light Being travels and blinks on the left side of the screen.

Tarantino, Q. (Director). (2015). *The Hateful Eight* [Motion picture on DVD]. USA: Anchor Bay Entertainment.

Ted, B. (n.d.). *'CHI' by Other Names Around the World*. Retrieved January 31, 2018, from http://www.neo-duddhism.org/chi-by-other-names-around-the-world.html

Tilly, T. (2018, February 13). *Your Daily Focus for February 14, 2018.* Retrieved March 8, 2018, from https://www.youtube.com/watch?v=0ib81SGMEQw. (Forty '40!' Light Beings Show Up Throughout Video on curtain at left side of screen.)

White, J. (1996) *UFOs – In Search of An Overview*, 59-60, 1996.

Vallee, J. (1989). *Passport to Magonia* (1st ed.). New York, NY: Sterling Publishing.

Woodford, C. (2017, August 10). *Piezoelectricity - How Does It Work? |What Is It Used For?* Retrieved March 08, 2018, from http://www.explainthatstuff.com/piezoelectricity.html

YouTube - (*Orbs Making Crop Circle*) - https://www.express.co.uk/news/weird/842579/UFO-crop-circle-made-ball-of-light-